Road Companion to Democracy and Meritocracy

Road Companion to Democracy and Meritocracy

(Further Essays from an African Perspective)

Godfrey B. Tangwa

Langaa Research & Publishing CIG
Mankon, Bamenda

Publisher:
Langaa RPCIG
Langaa Research & Publishing Common Initiative Group
P.O. Box 902 Mankon
Bamenda
North West Region
Cameroon
Langaagrp@gmail.com
www.langaa-rpcig.net

Distributed outside N. America by African Books Collective
orders@africanbookscollective.com
www.africanbookscollective.com

Distributed in N. America by Michigan State University Press
msupress@msu.edu
www.msupress.msu.edu

ISBN: 9956-616-70-2

DISCLAIMER

All views expressed in this publication are those of the author and
do not necessarily reflect the views of Langaa RPCIG.

Content

Part One

Part Two
In the Spirit of GOBATA

Dedication

In affectionate memory of Bernard Nsokika Fonlon (1924-1986) – "the genuine intellectual" – who did his best to bring rationality into public affairs in Cameroon.

Acknowledgement

I would like to thank the *Alexander von Humboldt Foundation* and my German academic friends and collaborators, Professors Eckhard Breitinger of the University of Bayreuth and Wilhelm Vossenkuhl of the University of Munich, for their continued interest in and encouragement of my work. I am inexpressibly grateful to Ulli and Georgia Beier and Elizabeth (Sally) M. Chilver for their incessant and multifarious help and encouragement. I thank GRAPHICAM, Yaounde, and especially Tobias Neba, for preparing a camera-ready copy for the publisher. I also thank KOLA TREE PRESS, Bellingham, USA, and especially Judith and Milton Krieger, for providing the context within which this publication became viable and particularly for their boldness in experimenting with unconventional publishing methods.

Preface

This book is a follow-up to my *DEMOCRACY AND MERITOCRACY: Philosophical Essays and Talks from an African Perspective* (Galda+ Wilch Verlag, Glienicke-Berlin, 1996). While preparing the manuscript of the latter, I discovered more material in my files, all broadly concerned with the same theme, than could be included in a single volume. The present book makes use of most of that material. The book is divided into two parts.

Part One comprises essays, articles and tit-bits, spanning roughly a decade, all revelatory of "the trouble with Cameroon" and my sustained but unfruitful efforts at tackling various aspects of the main underlying problem at the conceptual level. **Part Two** comprises the articles of my weekly column, *"In the Spirit of Gobata,"* published in the CAMEROON POST between July 1996 and June 1997.

All essays collected in this book are like random snap-shots, of varying degrees of sharpness, depicting various details on Cameron's rough and tedious journey to an unknown destination. They give me both the personal satisfaction of having tried, in the only way I knew how, to influence the evolution of things positively, and a sense of frustration at having failed.

As I am writing this Preface, the dictatorship in Cameroon, which, for nearly a decade, has been successfully impersonating a democracy, and which inspired most of the essays in this volume, has again successfully managed, against all odds and the democratic struggle, to maintain itself in power. In this situation, will Cameroonians invent new peaceful ways of sustaining the democratic/meritocratic struggle, will they allow hell to break loose on this beautiful triangle or will they simply give up the struggle and let dictatorship with a democratic mask dance unperturbed until it hopefully exhausts itself by its own dancing? I would no longer hazard a guess.

B.B.T., Yaounde, 03/11/1997

Part One

1

Democracy and Development in Africa: Putting the Horse before the Cart[1]*

Introduction
Before the colonial intervention in the history of Africa, the continent was politically composed of various Kingdoms (Fondoms), some of which were relatively large (e.g. Ghana, Songhai, Benin, Bornu, Sokoto) and others relatively small (e.g. Nso,' Bali Bafut, Kom). Sometimes these Kingdoms were at war against one another, but, for the most part, they cohabited quite peacefully. Within each Kingdom, the political system that predominated can perhaps best be described as a harmonious marriage between autocratic dictatorship and popular democracy. For while the King or Queen generally appeared very powerful (especially from outside) and his/her word could frequently condemn anyone to death, s/he was, nevertheless, subject to very strict control, not only by means of taboos but from institutions and personalities of very high moral authority and integrity whose main preoccupation was protection and safeguarding of the Kingdom as distinguished from the King, the interests of the ordinary person, the land, the ancestors and the unborn. Examples of the type of institutions and personalities alluded to here are, to take examples from my own natal background, *Nwerong* or *Kwifon, Yeenwerong, Nggang, Kighevshuu*, priests/priestesses, sages, and *Angaashiv* who usually combined the functions of medical doctor, priest, psychiatrist, psychologist and exorcist. These controls were an effective safeguard against dictatorial or arbitrary misuse and abuse of power and authority. The privileges and advantages of kingly power in Nso' arguably only balance, more or less, its responsibilities, restrictions and dangers.

In this situation it was not uncommon to witness the King/Queen publicly atoning for a mistake s/he had committed or a taboo s/he had wittingly or unwittingly broken. As recently as 1989, the Fon of Nso,' Ngga'Bi'fon III (1983-1993), performed such a public act of atonement at the instance of *Ngwerong*. The Nso' greatly revere and almost unquestioningly obey their King and concede extensive powers to him which are, however, considered as held in trust and reciprocity. The Nso' say: *Nso' dze Nso' bi Fon a Fon dze Fon bi Nso'* (The Nso' are what they are because of their King and the King is King because of the Nso'). As an institution, the Fon is considered immortal; he does not die, he only "disappears." As a person, however, the Fon is frequently reminded of his weakness and powerlessness and sometimes called

In some traditional African Kingdoms, the King/Queen could even be quietly executed or asked to voluntarily drink poison if his/her continued reign was considered dangerous for the survival and/or well-being of the Kingdom. It may not be very easy for people of western cultures to understand this state of affairs.

Today Africa can be aptly described as a crises-ridden continent: politically, economically, socially, environmentally, educationally, health-wise, etc. And yet Africa can equally well also be aptly described as the richest continent on earth: geographically, climatically, historically, culturally, linguistically, resource-wise, etc. Why is Africa so poor in spite of her riches? Is Africa poor *because of* her riches?

Wherever we turn today in Africa, we seem to encounter some disaster or catastrophe, natural or human-made, all mutually self reinforcing and self-sustaining: famine, drought, war, civil strife, epidemics, extreme poverty, mass unemployment, despair and hopelessness, etc. Now, where did Africa go wrong? At what point did she miss the road and how can she retrace her steps back onto the right path of development, prosperity, peace and tranquillity? My own proposal here is that Africa must first put together her political act, that is, install genuine democratic systems on firm and solid democratic structures before other good things could possibly follow. I subscribe to Nkwame Nkrumah's famous idea: *Seek first the political kingdom and other things shall follow!* Such democratic structures and systems can freely borrow from foreign systems and influences but should be founded and grounded on Africa's own traditional systems shorn of their undesirable elements and appropriately modernised.

The Monistic Tyrannies of Western Culture

Western political theory and practice would seem to be governed by an irreconcilable binary antagonism between dictatorship and democracy. In fact, the history of western philosophy in general is suffused and governed by binary thinking and antagonism between alternatives often conceived as mutually exclusive and irreconcilable: the One or the Many, Realism or Idealism, Universal or Particular, Matter or Mind, Rationalism or Empiricism, Egoism or Altruism, Autocracy or Democracy, Christianity or Islam, Catholicism or Protestantism, Capitalism or Socialism, Individualism or Communalism, Open Market or Planned Economy, Anthropocentricism or Biocentricism, Matriarchy or Patriarchy, etc.

One Western philosopher who has recently drawn attention to this "either –or" syndrome in western philosophy is Frederick Ferre[2]. The syndrome is related to what another western philosopher has characterised as a "transcendental pretence" -that is, a strong impulse to present western ideas, whether optimistic or pessimistic, *sub specie universali*, if not *sub specie aeternitati*, and as the only rational, and universally valid ones.[3] The syndrome has resulted in what one might call certain dogmatic monistic tyrannies (in rhyme with prevailing extreme individualism) which seem to govern western culture and world-view: the one and only true God (monotheism), one man one wife (monogamy), one morality, one people - one nation - one language, one civilisation, one world market, one world bank, one monetary fund, one and only way to development, one scientific method for attaining knowledge and/or truth etc.

The global dominance of western culture, thanks to its scientific-cum-technological success, seems to have reinforced the attitude that "might is right" and the inevitable arrogance that accompanies it on the side of the mighty. Since the Industrial Revolution, the strongest impulse and motive force of western culture has been the desire to know, co-ordinate, unify, harmonise, control, commercialise and monopolise everything on earth and even in the universe as a whole. As a corollary of this outlook, the western academic enterprise has been characteristically and centrally obsessed with the idea of "absolute certainty" among other closely connected categories. Western thinkers who have attempted to construct less certainty-ambitious systems, which might have helped to reduce or moderate western over-confidence and accompanying arrogance, have usually been disdainfully dismissed on the ground that the doubts on which they purport to base their system are themselves not certain enough. Karl Popper, for instance, who proposed a very simple and clear epistemological system based on ineradicable human limitations and fallibility, which could have helped to reduce or moderate the western quest for divine attributes, has usually been ignored or dismissed on the ground that his proposed fallibilism is itself fallible and hence not absolutely certain.

From nuclear accidents (Chernobyl 1986) to space rocket disasters (Challenger 1986), from city terrorism (Oklahoma City 1995) to mad-cow disease alias BSE/CJD (Jacob's Syndrome 1996) - the only health hazard in recent times whose origin western scientists have not yet traced to the African continent, from the Green House Effect to depletion of the ozone layer, the handwriting of the dangers of too much technology combined with too much arrogant certainty has been boldlywritten on the wall, but western culture has refused to read it.

Western culture does, of course, have its good points and advantages, but these are not my concern here and now.

By contrast to the monistic tyrannies of western culture, African cultures, world-views, systems of thought, religions and philosophies are united in their liberalism, live and let live attitude, non-aggressiveness, non-proselytizing character and in their harmonisation of the most varied diversities or peaceful cohabitation of the most apparently contradictory elements. The diversity of African languages, cultures, religions etc, is complimented by belief in and/or practice of monotheism/ polytheism (or rather polydivinity)/polydaemonism. monogamy/ polygamy/celibacy, African Traditional Religion/Islam/Christianity, etc. In Africa, it is not uncommon to find in a single household, peacefully cohabiting under the same roof, advocates of Communism, Capitalism, Catholicism, Protestantism, Islam, Bornagainism, Traditionalism, Atheism, etc. Pluralism and diversity are the hall marks of almost everything African. Such ideas as "ideological conformism," "genetic purity," "ethnic cleansing," etc, would have been unthinkable in traditional Africa. Tribalism and ethnicism which have wrecked havoc in many African countries in recent times are part and parcel of Africa's colonial legacy. Of course, African culture and systems are not without their own peculiar weaknesses and short-comings, since there is no coin without a reverse side, but these are not my concern here and now.

As there are no convincing arguments even in western philosophy itself for the existence or non-existence of, say, one God or many gods or no God at all, it is clear that only a certain attitude must have led to the view that western monotheism, for instance, is the natural culmination of all other religious conceptions, is superior to its putative rivals and universally valid. As J. Baird Callicott both queries and explains:

> Why should monotheism be regarded as any less primitive than animism? It apparently arose, at least in its familiar Judeo-Christian-Islamic form, largely because a single group of people insisted that their particular tribal divinity was superior to the one that their neighbours, such as the Canaanites, worshipped. The earlier biblical texts suggest that Yahweh considered himself to be one of many gods, ruling over one of many peoples, the Hebrews. As time went on, the Israelites elevated their god to the status of the only god[4].

As it may not be very easy for people who work exclusively within western academic paradigms to follow my arguments in this paper, let me make an initial specification which I have frequently found necessary and helpful in this regard. The generalisations that I make in this paper should not be taken to be of the Aristotelian logic type which any arm-chair academic can falsify with any single counter-instance. Most of my generalisations are of the type: "This is a bag of beans." which is not a claim about the total absence of a few pebbles that a diligent searcher might find among the beans in the bag. To say for instance, that *amala* and *ewedu* are the staple diet of the Yoruba people, is not to deny that they also eat roasted plantain with fresh palm oil. I am not out to construct a "system" of any sort. I am only addressing a concrete practical problem. When I talk of the kleptocratic dictatorships of Africa, it is not because I am unaware of Julius Nyerere or of South Africa and Nelson Mandela. I talk about what is typical without any implied claim that there are no exceptions, even if I don't mention them.

7

Dictatorships in Africa

It is the various colonial administrations which introduced pure dictatorships, that is, dictatorships without any controls or checks and balances, in Africa even at a time that die colonial so-called metropoles themselves were becoming more and more democratic. Some of Africa's traditional Kingdoms even started imitating aspects of the colonial system of governance before it became the dominant system of the post-independence regimes.

A single detailed example would show what I mean. When the Germans first arrived in my own home area, Nso,' in the Western Grassfields of Kamerun in 1902, they found a relatively flourishing and rapidly expanding Kingdom composed of originally much smaller kingdoms most of which had voluntarily merged and a few of which had been subdued and annexed by military force.

The King (Fon) of Nso,' who, by original consensus, was always selected by a committee headed by the leader of one of the strands comprising the Kingdom from among the male offspring of a female of another distinct strand (the *mntar* or free commoner class) and a male of yet another strand (the acknowledged royal *wonto'* or princes class), had very extensive powers which were, however, considered as held in trust and subject to several putative controls. The whole political set-up was such as to create a certain amount of stability and self-confidence. And one of the German officers, named Zimmermann, armourer to Captain Pavel, did not fail to note in writing that although the Nso' had never seen Europeans before, they were nevertheless "confident in their bearing unlike the timid forest people."[5] This, however, must have been considered an undesirable disposition, at least by Lt. Houben and his band who arrived Nso' barely 5 months after Pavel and his own group with many conscripts from other Grassfield Kingdoms, notably, Bali and Babungo. Failing to bully the leadership of the Nso' Kingdom into timidity, Houben and his band set the Nso' Palace (Nto[6] Nso') on fire after picking it clean of what they considered valuable before proceeding to Banyo.

Pavel himself had stated explicitly in writing that he and his retinue had been well received in Nso' and that the Fon (King) had agreed he would comply with their demands punctually.[7] But, that notwithstanding, the Germans returned to Nso' in 1905 under

Captain Houptmann Claiming. Commander of the Schutztruppc in the Bamenda *Bezirk* (District) and again attempted to intimidate the Nso' into submission by a demonstration march through all the states bordering Nso' proper - a veritable *argumentum ad bacculum*. The Fon, Sëëm II (1880 - 1907), was, however, unimpressed and is reported to have even boasted that he had nothing to fear because his subjects were as numerous as finger millet.'

Meanwhile, the Germans discovered that the Bamum Kingdom, ancestral brothers of the Nso,' had a serious grudge against the latter on account of their late King, Sangou (father of the then incumbent, Njoya) who, twenty years earlier, had been beheaded during a battle in Nso'. His skull was still retained in Nso' and according to traditional custom, a new King could not be properly enstooled (enthroned) in Bamum without it. So Glauning went into a strong alliance with the Bamum who saw here a golden opportunity not only to recover Sangou's skull but to avenge themselves against the Nso'. Using two well-equipped companies, Glauning's army and its Bamum allies invaded Nso in April 1906 from two directions. The war lasted exactly forty days during which canon and machine gun fire taught the Nso' how to be timid and how not to carry a confident bearing before Europeans. On June 6th 1906, Sëëm II admitted to Glauning: "Atav.ne shaamo." (You have proved stronger than I), and surrendered[8].

A few months later, the Germans summoned the Fon to Bamenda (c. 100 km. away) and insisted that he should come in person so as to impress it upon him where ultimate authority now lay and to arrange taxation of his people. Suppressing his pride and the premonitions of many of his subjects, he set out for Bamenda with a large entourage. He fell ill on the way and had to be carried in a litter made with the Nso' traditional royal cloth (Kilanglang). On arrival in Bamenda, a succession of very dramatic events occurred. Part of the opening testimony of the famous *Yaa wo Faa* who, as Queen-Mother (actually Sëëm II's) daughter who had succeeded his mother, Lirfee, as titular Queen-Mother after the latter's death), accompanied the

Fon to Bamenda, is worth quoting. *Yaa wo Faa,* whose pre-installation name was Kidzeru, had been captured by the Germans during the 40-day war and taken as booty to Yaounde. But after the capitulation, she was speedily retrieved with a heavy ransom (most probably in ivory). In 1916, *Yaa wo Faa* told Lawrence Fanka (later Ngga Bi'fon II) and Paul Mzeka, in the course of an interview:

> When we arrived at the station (i.e. Bamenda), a German Officer, quite a short man. came to meet the Fon. He welcomed him and asked whether he had brought some elephant tusks. Sëëm retorted: "Last year you almost finished all my people. Now you ask for elephant tusks. You say you are God, why don't you turn these to elephant tusks?" he asked pointing to his own teeth.[9]

Shortly afterwards, the Fon's illness intensified and a German doctor administered some treatment. But, by around mid-night he died and his entourage found themselves landed with the unprecedented heavy duty and burden of carrying his remains back to Nso'. Whether he died <u>consequent</u> or <u>subsequent</u> to the treatment he had received is an issue for open guess-work and controversy. One of the most plausible theories supporting the second option, and one to which *Yaa wo Faa* herself subscribed, is that he died out of distress at having violated an oft' repeated vow, before the advent of the Germans, to the effect that he, Sëëm, son of Lirfee and Taamanjo, would rather die than surrender to an enemy in any war. Opinions which support the first option often extrapolate from the future into the past by mentioning the actions of German doctors during the Second World War.

Writing about the expansion of the Nso' in the 19th and early 20th centuries, Mzeka N. Paul has noted tellingly that one of the factors which encouraged this expansion in both human and territorial terms was

> ...the tendency to use the strategy of consensus rather than coercion in administrative pursuits- Pre-German survivors in Nso' insist that coercive use of authority in certain areas of Nso' culture was imitated from the German colonial administration, which used physical force as an instrument of administration.[10]

After independence, Africans inherited the dictatorial systems and structures of colonialism which they tried to justify by appeal to the need for national unity, integration, development, well-being and prosperity. But this was evidently simply an immunizing tactic of colonialism as it transformed itself into neo-colonialism and went into alliance with crafty individual Africans or a handful of such individuals so that economic exploitation of the continent could continue on a scale little different from that under overt colonialism. African post-colonial dictatorships are completely different from the pre-colonial kingships in their total lack of the democratic component, that is to say, checks and balances on behalf of or accountability to the people. Those who claim that the post-colonial dictatorships in Africa are modelled on traditional kingship have not taken account of this fact. Nowhere in traditional Africa could the king or queen be a public thief or some other such moral leper, under pain of dethronement or even execution. So stringent were the demands for upright moral behaviour. But how does it come about that contemporary African leaders, including all the dictators, with only a few putative exceptions, have been qualmless kleptocrats, most of whom have constantly emptied the public treasury of their impoverished countries to bank or invest abroad? The answer does not lie in dictatorship as such but in dictatorship without any controls, internal or external.

Stories about financial improprieties and corruption among public figures in western countries indicate that only strong disincentives can prevent people in power anywhere from the temptations of abuse of power for personal gain. In the western democracies, freedom of the press and the independence of the courts make the risk of exposure a strong, though not always sufficient disincentive to official or executive kleptocracy. But some of these people, who would if they really could, then go into alliance with African dictators who are accountable to no one but themselves and, in this way, they achieve, thanks to Africa, what they could not achieve at home.

It is no secret that the prosperity of the industrialised world owes a great deal to the Third World, particularly Africa. During the "Copenhagen Summit" (March 1995), Francois Mitterrand, then still president of France, criticising naked capitalism, is reported to have asked the following very apposite rhetorical question: "Are we really going to let the world become a global market without any rules other than those of the jungle and with no purpose other than maximum gain, maximum profit, in the minimum time?"[11] But Mitterrand probably asked this excellent rhetorical question, as some newspaper commentator remarked, just for the attention of his biographers. For how can such concern be reconciled with the fact that in Cameroon, for example, his own son is one of those who got a mandate as a special favour to destroy most of what still remains of Cameroon's forests in the name of exploiting for tropical wood?

When a new French president (Jacques Chirac) was elected recently (May 1995), I searched in the French press to find out what informed opinion might have to say about the prospect for Africa under a new leadership in France. Quite interestingly, I discovered that many of the commentators were predicting a very bright future for African countries within the "sphere of French influence" on the basis of the excellent *"relations personelles qu'il* (i.e. Chirac) *entretient depuis longtemps avec de nombreux chefs d'Etat de la region"*[12]. But personal relations between heads of state have absolutely nothing to do with it. If that is all there is to base our hopes and optimism on, then there is no doubt that the new French president, like all his other predecessors in office, would help to maintain francophone African dictators in power and aid and abate them as usual in the economic wreck and rape of their impoverished countries. A common denominator of European regimes of all political persuasions would seem to be continued exploitation of Africa.

In the early 1990's, following what was then called "the wind of change blowing from Eastern Europe," there was great optimism all over Africa that the dictatorships were about to give way to more democratic forms of governance. Most of the western democracies promised that they would no longer support dictatorial regimes. But today, the same dictatorships are going strong all over Africa because the promises were not kept. The promises were broken because of the special relationships that already existed with incumbent dictators or because it was not clear whether new democratic regimes, if allowed to come into power, would maintain existing economic arrangements. The case of South Africa, where a truly democratic miracle occurred, proves that, with enough sincerity and commitment from the western democracies, all African dictatorships would easily yield place to veritable democracies.

Kamerun: A Pocket Edition of Africa

Kamerun is really like a pocket edition of Africa, a veritable *Africa in Miniature*, as it is often called. Kamerun is like the meeting hall of nearly all the colonial legacies of Africa. First colonised by the Germans, it subsequently passed under the colonial administrative control of England and France. It is not at all surprising that all of Africa's macro-problems as well as its potentialities and positive possibilities are all present, to scale, in Kamerun.

The geographical, biological, historical, cultural and linguistic diversity of Kamerun is paradigmatic of the rest of Africa. The major ecosystems and climatic zones, the flora and fauna, as well as all the different shades of the black race, are all well represented in Kamerun. The over 12 million population of Kamerun is also composed of almost equal proportions of Traditionalists (40%), Christian converts (39%) and Islamists (21 %) - an ideal example of that triple heritage to which Nkrumah and Ali Mazrui have drawn so much attention, where Traditional African, Euro-Christian and Islamic values and influences are in forced marriage, for better or for worse.

From the economic angle, Kamerun is self-sufficient in domestic food production and produces in exportable quantities most of what is produced elsewhere in Africa: cocoa, coffee, tea, banana, groundnut, palm-produce, cotton, timber, rubber, petroleum, etc. With 236 indigenous languages and corresponding ethnic groups, and with French and English as official national languages, Africa's rich linguistic and cultural diversity finds nothing if not remarkable instantiation in Kamerun.

But, in spite of this profile, in spite of its tally remarkable human, natural and cultural resources, potentialities and possibilities, Kamerun is today one of Africa's spectacular cases of woeful failure: economically, politically, socially, etc. The reasons for this failure are not far to fetch; they have their foundation, origin and explanation in two successive dictatorships which have misruled Kamerun since the ostensible withdrawal of the colonial masters/

exploiters. The first of these dictatorships, under Ahmadou Ahidjo (up to 1982), was remarkably ruthlessly repressive while the second, under Paul Biya (1982—?) is remarkably qualmlessly and shamelessly kleptocratic.

Kamerun's economy, which a few decades ago was generally rated by experts as one of the most promising on the entire African continent, has been completely ruined by shady mismanagement, large-scale executive fraud and unbridled official thievery. Politically, Kamerun has remained in a virtual state of stalemate since 1992, when the ruling regime lost the first ever democratic presidential elections but decided, with the support of its French mentors and manipulators, who seemed afraid that their interest would not be protected under a democratic regime, to stay put in power. French policy in Africa is no secret to anybody. In stark terms, the French, by contrast with their other comrades in colonialism and empire-building, have never really uncolonised their own territories where the others, at least, did so by substitution with a remote-control arrangement. In Nigeria, the ugly giant of Africa, Kamerun's western neighbour, for instance, the British colonial masters did really depart at independence, although they sowed the bad seed whose poisonous fruits are being abundantly harvested today, by rigging the first democratic elections to ensure that "northerners" whom they considered more easily manipulate-able assumed political power at the centre. Anyone who has read the widely circulated but generally ignored letters of Harold Smith, a former colonial administrator in Nigeria, knows this fact. But in all French colonies, "independence" was simply a euphemism for an unbelievable political fraud and deception.

The current dictatorship in Kamerun stands out from its other African counter parts in its very skilful use of democratic vocabulary and rhetoric, even going as far as shamelessly describing itself as an "advanced democracy."

Kamerun has a standing dispute, which occasionally breaks out in open armed conflict, with its big neighbour, Nigeria, over the oil-rich Bakassi Peninsular. It is very significant to note that, before the discovery of petroleum in the area, there was no dispute and that each of the colonial masters necessarily implicated in the conflict as the original partitioners of the land and actual exploiters

14

and beneficiaries of the oil, support both sides in the conflict. Furthermore, Kamerun is also in real danger of internal conflict as the Anglophone minority component of the country (formerly "Southern Cameroons"), which united with "La Republique du Cameroun" in 1961 following a UN - conducted plebiscite, fed up with marginalisation, exploitation, neglect, repression, brutalization, continuing attempts at assimilation into the Francophonie and failure of its bold attempts to spear-head "democratisation, is threatening and poised to reassert its autonomy.

Democracy and Development

The post - independence regimes of African countries have been dismal failures although that is not to say that they have all failed to the same degree. Some of these dictatorships have brought their countries not only economic chaos and generalised misery but the real prospect of catastrophic collapse or disintegration. In some cases these African countries are worse off than they were under full blown colonialism and it is not surprising that some people in their exasperation have called for the return of the colonial masters.

It is quite clear that there would be no development in Africa nor even peace and tranquillity until the present dictatorships, some of which are successfully masquerading under democratic garb and rhetoric, yield place to genuinely democratic systems. This being the case, it goes without saying, that western governments or agencies which genuinely want to help Africa would do better to concentrate their efforts on helping to bring about genuine democracies in Africa rather than, say, giving economic aid and/or loans. It is a fact that in some cases money given as aid or loans to African countries has never left the west but simply changed banks, and yet future generations of Africans have inherited a heavy debt burden with nothing that can be shown as its justification. In helping Africa to democratise its governing systems, it is much more important to pay attention to the instauration of democratic structures, beginning with a broadly consensual constitution and electoral code, rather than to organising mere democratic elections. What recent experience has shown is that, without firm democratic structures, elections alone, be they ever so democratic, may, at best, only help in replacing one tyrant with another or, more usually, in confirming the incumbent tyrant in his monarchic office. As one very perceptive "outsider" has observed regarding the recent wave of multi-party elections in Africa:

> There is little difference between Arap Moi before and after the multi-party election. Chiluba, the democratically elected president of Zambia, uses against Kaunda similar repressive measures on the basis of the same emergency regulations used by Kaunda against him. And there was... the Nigerian case where the incumbents simply refused to abide by the election results. This is so because at the root of the problem lies not the lack of democratic elections but rather the highly monocentric, centralised, indeed, authoritarian governing system.[13]

No country can develop which does not mobilise or at least stimulate the popular energies of its own citizens towards constructive work and patriotic sacrifices. The most basic difference between a dictatorship and a democracy is that the former relies on one person's wisdom whereas the latter relies on the collective wisdom of all the members of the society. But to rely on a single individual's wisdom, no matter how powerful, knowledgeable and well intentioned s/he might be, is to choose the ditch for a destination, sooner or later. Whereas, collective wisdom, no matter how slow and conservative it might seem to be, is what can and has guided various communities to survive and develop through changing times and the inscrutable surprises of history.

In its classical conception in the western tradition, going back to Plato and the other ancient Greek philosophers, democracy is understood as the "rule of the people" or, as put in modern popular jargon, "government of the people, for the people, by the people." The people, of course, never govern or rule directly. And Sir Karl Popper in his book *The Open Society and Its Enemies*[14] makes a very illuminating contribution to democratic theory by suggesting that we should look on democracy not as "government of the people" but rather as any system which permits bad or unsuitable rulers or leaders who have outlived their usefulness to be "got rid of without bloodshed, without violence." Democracy in Africa need not follow exactly western models (some of whose elements, in fact, are only dubiously democratic) as long as it is built on the irreducible minimum condition of incorporating a system by which a bad government, or in any case, one perceived as such by the governed, can be easily removed and replaced without bloodshed or violence.

Democracy can also be viewed as a system of interconnected *values* and the *institutions* which promote and sustain those values. The classic values that have been associated with democracy are *liberty* and *equality* promoted and sustained, within the western world, by such institutions as courts and the press. Professor Leslie Lipson[15] has compared liberty and equality within democratic theory to space and time within theoretical physics. And just like space and time within theoretical physics, liberty and equality within political theory raise some conceptual perplexities. From a certain perspective, liberty and equality can be considered as opposites in the sense that they contradict each other when pushed to their logical limits. Liberty might be considered as an individualistic virtue and equality as a social one. Within western "binary thinking" those who are called "Rightists" have usually overemphasised freedom while "Leftists" overemphasise equality. The same emphatic prejudice underlies the difference between capitalism and socialism, respectively.

In fact, from a purely theoretical viewpoint, both liberty and equality can be considered as being internally contradictor. For example, liberty or freedom has both a positive and a negative connotation. We speak of "freedom to" (positive) as well as "freedom from" (negative). My freedom to swing my arms around comes up against the freedom of the person sitting next to me <u>from</u> the harmful effects of my freely swinging arms. In other words, freedom in the negative sense collides with freedom in the positive sense if both are affirmed as logical absolutes. Similarly, equality has different connotations. It might signify either uniformity or proportion. Do we treat people equally when we assign them exactly the same amount or different amounts? Should a child's share of food at table be exactly the same as that of the adult? Should every citizen pay only poll tax? How do we justify different treatment of what we conceive as equal or conceive as equal what can justifiably be treated differently? Moreover, equality, however conceived, is not provable. It is simply a moral imperative.

However, real life is not lived on the logical extremities of theory. In practice, as already mentioned, African systems of thought have little problem living with logical contradictions, and in western philosophy, following the <u>Aristotelian mean</u> can rescue us out of a lot of quandaries. Real life is best lived mid-way between several opposite extremes. Everyone has an equal right to express his/her opinion but that does not mean that all opinions are equally right. Freely expressed opinions must be considered and evaluated on their <u>merits.</u> Give an equal capital of say 100,000 francs to three "'equal" youngsters today and, by tomorrow, you may discover that one has finished squandering his own with prostitutes and *akwara* women, another has very profitably invested his while the third may still have his intact locked up in a tin. An equal starting point would thus, in practice, always give us very unequal results.

It is thus necessary to marry or coalesce freedom and equality in a manner very similar to what Einstein did in the realm of physics when he combined space and time into a single space-time concept. When we combine freedom and equality -which fundamentally are moral imperative - the idea that results is that of <u>equality of opportunity,</u> not equality of achievement or results. But, our moral sensibilities, will compel us to tinker with the unequal results so that both freedom and equality may not be annihilated for some. Julius Nyerere, the father of Ujamaa, very often described socialism as a system by which the inequalities in society are organised so as to achieve human equality. The recent collapse of the socialist systems of Eastern Europe would seem to signal the triumph of capitalism over socialism. But as the evils of capitalist "liberal economics" which depend purely on "market forces" are appreciated, the virtues of socialism would surely be rediscovered. But, for Africa at any rate, it is clear that whatever economic system may be deemed appropriate would have to be preceded by the instauration of genuine democracy and that none stands any chance of functioning without it.

Notes

1.* This paper was read on my behalf during the SUNY conference on "Philosophy, Politics, and Development in Africa: Assessing the Twentieth Century, and Looking Forward." Binghamton University, USA, June 7-9, 1996. Earlier versions had been read by me at a special lecture at the University of Munich (12/07/9 5) and at a staff/graduate-student seminar al the University of Wales Cardiff, U.K., (09/11/1995). The same paper was recently read by me at the *Premier Collogue Tricontinental de Philosophie.* Abidjan, Cote d'Ivoire. March 19 -22, 1997. *"Kimforkir"* (His Royal Fragility) behind his back. This attitude is clearly symbolised and ritualised during the burial ceremony of the Fon, when he is seated upright on a throne in the grave, uncapped, and his personal name, which could no longer be called from the moment of his installation, pronounced, with the addition that that is the person who has died, but that the Fon has not passed away and continues shining like the sun.

2. See Frederick Ferre, "Personalistic Organicism: Paradox or Paradigm?" - paper read during the Royal Institute of Philosophy Conference on "Philosophy and the Natural Environment," Cardiff, Wales. July 20-22, 1993.

3. See Robert. C, Solomon, *History and Human Nature: A Philosophical Review of European Philosophy and Culture 1750- 1850*, Brighton, Sussex, The Harvester Press, 1980.

4. J. Baird Callicott, *Earth's Insights: A Survey of Ecological Ethics from the Mediterranean Basin to the Australian Outback*, Berkeley, Los Angeles and London, University of California Press, 1994.

5. See Mzcka N. Paul, *Four Fons of Nso': Nineteenth and Early Twentieth Century Kingship in the Western Grassfields*, Bamenda, The Spider Publishing Enterprise, 1990, p. 77: quoting E.M. Chilver, Nso' and the Germans (unpublished field research notes), p.l.

6. ' ibid., p. 78.

7. ibid., p. 77. Said Sëëm II, while releasing a fist full of finger millet through his fingers,: *Mfan Kaav? Amo Nso' dzeen ben!*" (What need I fear? Nso' people are like this!)

8. ibid., p. 79.

9. ibid- p.88

10. ibid-p- 15.

11. See *The Guardian*, 13 March 1993 and the *Anarchist Fortnightly, FREEDOM, 25* March 1395.

12. See for instance, "Le Nouveau Visage da la France?" in *Jeune Afrique*, No. 1792. 11-17 Mai 1995.

13. Mordechai Tamarkin, "Culture, Stale and Politics in Africa; 'Tribalism' or Moral Ethnicity," unpublished paper read during an international conference under the theme: *"Breaking the Boundaries: Beyond the Land of Cush- New Critical Encounters with Languages and Literatures of Sub-Saharan Africa*, Tel Aviv University, 18-23 June 1995, pp. 10-11.

14. Karl R. Popper, *The Open Society and Its Enemies* (vol. I: *The Spell of Plato: Vol. II: The High Tide of Prophecy: Hegel, Marx, and the Aftermath*, London and Henley, Routledge and Kegan Paul. 1945.

15. Leslie Lipson, "The Philosophy of Democracy" in *Dialogue*, NO 72.2

2

The Medium and Long Term Lessons of the Lake Nyos Natural Disaster[1]*

There have been three events in recent times that have drawn world-wide attention to Cameroon, a country which, otherwise, might have been thought to be practising *quietism* as its own official ideology. The first of these three events that I have in mind was the 1982 'World Cup' in Spain where Cameroon's 'Indomitable Lions' - one of the two highly underrated African teams - performed quite creditably. The second event was the 1984 abortive putsch in which a bunch of soldiers dropped a rock into the usually serene political waters of a nation whose political stability had become the envy of its neighbours. The third event is the August 21st, 1986, Lake Nyos natural disaster.

The first of these three events chronicled above was a pride to all Cameroonians, the second was a veritable embarrassment, and the third is pure anguish.

Before it ends, 1986 might qualify as the Century's Year of Greatest Disasters. This year we have heard of earthquakes, landslides, famine, nuclear plant accidents, industrial gas leakages, plane crashes, ship sinkings, rocket explosions, city bombings and daily plain shootings. Thousands of human lives have perished and continue to perish.

All these disasters might be categorised under two headings: those due to natural causes and those due to human agency, although some overlap must be admitted for some of the cases. Now, while disasters in the second category are avoidable and can conceivably be completely eliminated from our world via tolerance, understanding and sheer common sense, disasters in the first category are not usually avoidable nor can they be completely eliminated, although their deleterious effects can certainly be minimized.

It is therefore important to reflect on the Lake Nyos natural disaster, in which an estimated 2000 of our compatriots perished, in order to see what lessons we might learn from it.

The first thing that must be understood *ab initio* is that our knowledge of the world and of all natural phenomena in general is, at best, in the form of intelligent guesses. Nature is completely inert, having neither feelings nor emotions nor arms nor purposes. And because we human beings have aims and purposes, feelings and emotions, nature stands as an adversary against us - indomitable, invincible and - inexorably cruel. While as human beings we always act purposively, for good or ill, nature, by contrast, is mostly incomprehensibly capricious in its actions. This is why, from his earliest beginnings, man has sought to understand, to control and thereby gain dominion over nature It is, however, evident that nature cannot be understood beyond a certain extent nor can it be tamed in the manner in which some wild animals have been domesticated by man. Human aims and purposes constantly flounder against nature. Indeed, to borrow an expression from David Hume, the Scottish philosopher (1711 - 1776), "Nature is always too strong for principle."

The reason that our knowledge of nature, that is to say, our scientific knowledge in the broadest sense, can never be better than intelligent conjectures or hypotheses or guesses is that we can only learn about nature through experience. And since experience can only be corrected by further experience we have no guarantee that our experiential knowledge of today might not be rendered untenable by future experience. In other words, the knowledge that we have of nature depends on our past observations, our past experience. But we have no guarantee that the future will be like the past. Why may things not suddenly change? This is why it has been rightly said that even if we had complete and correct knowledge about nature we would not even be able to know that we had it.

This is the general philosophical background to the assertion that the best we can hope to achieve in the realm of nature are intelligent guesses. There are, for instance, several hypotheses as to what exactly happened at Lake Nyos on that fateful night of August 21st. What caused the explosion? A gas? Was it a single gas or a combination of gases? What gas caused the deaths? Was it carbon dioxide, carbon monoxide, hydrogen sulphide or sulphur dioxide, etc'. Some of the suggested hypotheses can easily be ruled out with good arguments. In this way we might end up with one hypothesis which is most resilient against all criticism and argument. We would then adopt such a hypothesis as the most likely, but there is no way we can be absolutely sure of its correctness. What, in fact, we might be quite certain about are those hypotheses which are incorrect. We must therefore hold our 'correct' hypothesis tentatively, leaving open the possibility of its being shown to have been false after all. This means that our projects can never really be completed. There will never be a time that we can rest on our oars fully satisfied. This also shows that our knowledge in these matters can only grow in a rather negative fashion. We get to know what is not the case, but we can never be absolutely sure of what is the case. We are sure of the wrong hypotheses (through arguments and criticism) but we can never be absolutely sure that the hypothesis we entertain or adopt is the correct one. This also shows, incidentally, that in this realm mistakes and wrong hypotheses or conjectures are important because they help to increase our knowledge, albeit, negatively. This situation ought to foster a sense of humility in all humankind.

Now with regard to the Lake Nyos disaster certain broad hypotheses can easily be ruled out. For instance, the disaster was certainly not caused by the witchcraft of certain individuals within the unfortunate community, nor was it caused by the malevolence of any of their neighbours. The disaster was certainly not an eschatological "armageddon" of which some bible-rattling Christians warn us daily, nor was it due to God's anger for some abominable sin committed. If these implicit hypotheses 1 am here dismissing seem far fetched, let me say that 1 have heard a Cameroonian react to news of the disaster with the following ejaculatory expression: "I swear, those Menchum people get bad witch!" And a 'born again" undergraduate student of mine here at the University of Ife assures me that the only solution to the problem and insurance against any reoccurrence is to 'accept Jesus'.

The disaster certainly had a natural cause connected with volcanic action although the precise cause must remain a subject for scientific conjecture. We must therefore first rule out all superstitious and supernatural explanations. Incantations or sacrifices or exorcism will not prevent a recurrence of the disaster; neither will prayer, fasting and repentance or acceptances of Jesus, although these might well be quite appropriate for other reasons.

The reality of our situation is that we live in a country which is geologically mountainous and prone to volcanic action. We must therefore take full cognizance of this in our attempts to understand, control and harness the natural phenomena of our environment for our survival and well being.

Within the present century, volcanic occurrences have been recorded in Cameroon during the following years: 1909, 1922, 1954, 1959, 1966, 1977, 1980, 1982, 1984, 1986. Within the last decade these eruptions have assumed a biennial sequence. Some have argued from this that the next year to watch with careful apprehension would be 1988. But this is superstitious thinking inasmuch as it implicitly confers purposive or intelligent action to blind inanimate forces. There is no order in nature except that which can be discerned only from hindsight. There is therefore no guarantee against another volcanic action this very year nor should it be surprising if our volcanoes go dormant for the next decade or even century. We cannot therefore afford ever to relax our vigilance.

It is thus disappointingly significant that even after the Lake Manoun episode of only two years ago in which 37 lives were lost, the only seismograph which could have given warning of the latest disaster is said to have been out of order. We must also cast a critical reflective eye at the fact that news of the Nyos disaster took a long time to filter through because of the *inaccessibility of the area.* In short, news of the disaster reached outside the disaster area through the agency of eye witnesses whose mode of communication was personal locomotion *cum pedibus.* There are neither telephones nor electricity nor a viable motor road to this part of our country. Over 25 years after political independence, what we call the "Ring Road," which is the most important communication link in the whole province, is, in many respects, in a worsecondition than it was during the colonial era.

Because of this problem of inaccessibility, relief could not get to the survivors as quickly as might otherwise have been the case; and who knows how many might have died simply because of this factor? It is for the same reason that President Paul Biya who rushed to Bamenda immediately on getting news of the disaster was unable to get to the stricken area and had to make do with observing it from the air.

A situation where any part of our country is inaccessible is certainly unsatisfactory and we must address ourselves to this problem. The process of rural development and modernization must also be given a new impetus. And in this connection good roads are the first indispensable requirement.

There is good reason for us to be apprehensive of a Lake Nyos-type of action on other lakes in Cameroon. These include Lakes Oku, Bambuliwe, Barombikang, Manenguba and, of course, Monoun. These must not only be constantly monitored but a resettlement scheme must be carefully worked out for all who dwell within, say, a ten kilometre radius from any of these potentially dangerous lakes.

A resettlement scheme - that is, getting people to permanently leave an area where their economic, social and cultural life has been lived - is never an easy project to execute. But here we can solicit the help of those friendly nations which so kindly rushed to our aid during the recent emergency. According to reports, such countries included Israel, Britain, France, USA, Germany and Nigeria. However, all our efforts must be spearheaded and co-ordinated by Cameroonians. For no nation can hope to survive, much less achieve self-reliance and well being solely through the humanitarianism and philanthropism of other nations.

The Lake Nyos disaster is a great challenge to Cameroonian scholars, researchers and policy makers. It offers both an opportunity and an incentive for *relevant* research and patriotic commitment. It can only be hoped that they would prove equal to this challenge.

Note

1.* This paper was written on 09/09/86 at the University of Ife (now Obafemi Awolowo University), Nigeria, where I was a Philosophy Lecturer cum graduate student from 1978 -1986, and published in *CAMEROON TRIBUNE* of Tuesday, October 28, 1986.

3

X For All by the Year 2000[1]

The year 2000 A.D. ought to be designated the "International Year of Hope." Nearly everyone is familiar with the expression 'Health for all by the year 2000" which has been popularized as the campaign slogan of the World Health Organisation (W.H.O.). But other goodies apart from health have also been promised to an ever expectant humanity by the year 2000. We have also heard of peace and safety for all by the year 2000, food and shelter for all by the year 2000, justice and fair play for all by the year 200 employment for all by the year 2000, literacy for all by the year 2000, etc.

These slogans are symptomatic of very high hopes indeed. They indicate deep human aspirations. Human beings cannot but aspire towards the good as they perceive it. But human hopes must have some justification if they are not to be vain. In other words, we might desire a certain state of affairs to exist. And no one can be blamed for his desires since they are spontaneous and involuntary. Desires are things that happen to us rather than things that we do. We have no control over our desires. So we cannot be praised or blamed, or, in any way, held responsible for them. But to expect a certain state of affairs to exist requires reasons and a justification for the expectation. One may; for instance, desire to be the most knowledgeable person on earth. But one cannot hope, that is, expect to achieve this state of affairs, without any learning which is the only way by which human beings acquire knowledge. To do so would be to have a vain hope doomed to certain failure.

Now our desires for the year 2000 stand in need of no justification. We owe no one any apologies for them. They are simply manifestations of our human nature which aspires spontaneously towards the good as perceived by us.

But to go from mere aspiration to expectation or hope requires justification. Now, are our hopes for the year 2000 justified?

The year 2000 is, no doubt, a very- significant one. It marks not only the end of a century but also the end of a millennium. And every end signifies also a new beginning. It is therefore understandable that humanity should be aspiring towards a new beginning that marks the end of disease and hunger, of injustice and strife, of poverty and want that have characterised the better part of the present century and, indeed, of the entire millennium.

But let us, with cold realism, look at some of our aspirations for the year 2000 to see whether we are justified in hoping for these things. The first thing to note is that, though it sounds so far away, the year 2000 is little more than a decade away, precisely, it is only some thirteen years away. And a realistic way to calculate what might obtain in the affairs of men in 13 years' time is to compare the present state of affairs with the situation 13 years ago. Subtract the situation 13 years ago from what obtains today and add the result to the present state of affairs and the answer would be, *mutatis mutandis,* what would obtain 13 years hence.

Let us limit ourselves to Cameroon and to health which is getting a well co-ordinated campaign. Can Cameroon realistically hope to achieve health for all its citizens by the year 2000?

There has, no doubt, been a great improvement in our health care delivery system in the last decade or so. More hospitals and health centres have been built and more medical personnel trained. Health is one area where Cameroon is presently blessed with a dynamic minister who understands not only what health care is all about but also that it is a right for all Cameroonians rather than a privilege for the rich and powerful few. Here indeed is one minster who dearly seems to fulfil President Biya's desire that the ministers he appoints should be *responsible.* Nevertheless, a minister, no matter how clear-sighted, dynamic and hard-working, cannot, by his efforts alone, hope to change beliefs, attitudes and practices that have crystallized over several years. The active co-operation of all medical personal and the public at large is indispensable. Health for all would remain only a sweet dream unless and until all medical personnel approach their functions with that moral sensibility which regards all human life as supremely valuable and all human beings as equal in their health needs. The general public must also take seriously its own health at the primary level. It is amazing, for instance, that, in spite of the facilities available, many Camerounians leave much to be desired with regard to their personal hygiene and nutrition. Many people voluntarily choose to live in filthy surroundings and, in spite of relatively abundant availability of food, many are malnourished via over-eating and poor dieting. One amusing way in which our 'landscape' is changing is that quite often these days when approaching a "well-to-do" citizen from afar you frequently get the strong impression that an expectant mother is coming your way. Somehow I cannot recall ever seeing any of these 'pregnant men' while growing up around the fifties and early sixties.

Carefully considered, therefore, we must conclude that "health for all by the year 2000" is, for us, no more than a magnificent prescriptive objective. It is an objective which we cannot realistically hope to achieve unless our society undergoes a transformation that would be close to miraculous. That is not to say, however, that the objective is not worth striving for. Only that, in an age when empty slogans frequently take the place of purposive action, we should be careful lest we mistake *form* for *matter*.

And if we cannot realistically hope to achieve health for all by the year 2000, then need we say more again about the other anticipated components of the good life? We certainly need no fortune teller to reveal to us that, come the year 2000, we would continue to be beset by all the problems now plaguing us. The rich and powerful amongst us would have grown richer and more powerful and the poor (who survive) would be poorer and more wretched. By the year 2000, our cities would still be demarcated into posh areas reserved for the chosen few and shanty slum areas for the *massa damnata,* the Fanonian wretched of the earth. In the year 2000, the "dossiers" of poor and unknown individuals will continue to get lost in the ministries. Come the year 2000, it will still be near-impossible, as it was and is, for the unknown child of an unknown peasant, however qualified, to get a job within our system. Good jobs will continue to be reserved for those in power and their relations and tribesmen and friends. In the year 2000, the majority of Cameroonians will continue to see illusory visions and to dream dreams.

One is no prophet for the year 2000. But these are no predictions. These are certified certainties extrapolated from present realities. Unless, of course, someone *responsible* were to will that it should be otherwise and to demand that it must be.

Note

1. This paper was written while I was jobless in Cameroon and published in *CAMEROON TRIBUNE* of Friday January 2, 1987.

4

Letter to the Dean[1]

C/O Mr. John MBIYBE
Caisse d 'Epargne Postal du
Cameroun, Yaounde,
19/1/87

The Dean
Faculty of Letters and Social Sciences
University of Yaounde
Yaounde

Dear Sir,

Appeal for a review of my candidature for recruitment as a lecturer in the Dept, of Philosophy.

BACKGROUND:

I first applied to the University for a lectureship in November 1984, immedi-ately after obtaining my Ph D. from the University of Ibadan, upon learning that the University of Yaounde was in fact in need of a lecturer of my qualification and calibre in philosophy.

Subsequently, I received a letter from the Chancellor's office, dated 8th January, 1885, and signed by Mr. C. MBOM, acknowledging receipt of my application and listing a series of documents which I should supply to the Chancellor's office.

On February 12th, I answered the above letter and complied with all its demands.

After this I did not hear anything again from the University for several months. So, I came over from Nigeria in October, 1985, to find out what the situation was. It was then I learnt that a new policy was in force which required all vacant positions to be first advertised before recruitment and that my application would have to await such advertisement before it could be considered.

An advertisement by the Chancellor duly appeared in the Cameroon Tribune of February 26th 1986 listing *inter alia,* vacancies in the Dept. of philosophy in areas including Epistemology and Logic. Upon reading this advertisement, I again came over from Nigeria in April 1986, and reinforced my application with my letter of April 2nd, and certified true copies of ail my certificates which I had earlier sub-mitted in photocopies.

About June, 1986, MANGA-BIHINA, the Head of the Philosophy Depart-ment, got me informed through Dr. G.V. Fanso of the History Department, that my recruitment was impending as it had already been favourably recommended, await-ing only the approval of the final recruitment commission and that I should therefore ensure that I was free for the coming academic session.

Although I don't have Dr. Fanso's letter here with me, having left it back in Nigeria, both he and Mr. MANGA-B1HINA are here and can confirm this point.

On receiving the above information, I considered it my patriotic duty to terminate my lectureship appointment at the University of Ife and accordingly handed in a three month's notice of resignation as was required by the rules of my appoint-ment there.

I am by no means implying here I should have been recruited simply on the grounds that I had unwittingly been caused to resign my appointment prematurely in anticipation of being recruited. The fact, however, is that this unfortunate turn of events has rendered me completely jobless since October 1986, with severe conse-quences for my family and dependents.

It was in October last year that I got here and was shocked to discover that the University Commission did not in fact recruit me. I went to see the Head of the Philosophy Dept, to find out why I was not recruited. He told me he too had been surprised that I was not recruited but that, not being a member of the recruitment commission, he had no idea as to why I was not recruited. He advised me to see the Dean of the Faculty. And, you would recall, Sir, that on Saturday, 11th October, 1986, I did come to see you and you told me that you were not present at the commis-sion when my case was discussed and that I should go and see the Vice Chancellor to find out why I had not been recruited. You also told me that if there was no "'funda-mental reason" why the commission did not recruit me, I could be taken on provision-ally pending a review of my candidature.

When I went to the Vice Chancellor, he told me that the information I was seeking from him ought to be given to me by the Dean of the Faculty. He however, directed me to an officer in the Chancellery, Mr. BELA, who, after consulting some documents, told me that he believed the Commission did not recruit me for two main reasons:

(1) That extracts of my publications were not available;

(2) That my specialty, Epistemology and Metaphysics, was not what the de-partment really required. He also expressed the view that if extracts of my publica-tions had been available, the commission's decision might have been different.

This greatly surprised me because I had earlier sent extracts of all my publications and because, from the Chancellor's advertisement of 26th February, 1986, and from what the Head of the Philosophy Dept. had constantly told me, one of the areas in which the Department of Philosophy was greatly in need was Epistemology.

On Monday, November 24th, 1986, I sought to know from an officer at the Chancellery what I ought to do so that the case for my recruitment could be reviewed. I learnt that there was in fact a review meeting the very next day and that if I could make available extracts of the publications which had been said to be missing to the Dean of Letters and Social Sciences, he could make a case on my behalf at the meeting.

You would remember, Sir, that I did bring these documents to you that same day. But you said I should go and give them to the Head of the Philosophy Depart-ment. The Head of the Philosophy Department, however, told me that, as he was not a member of the commission and could not therefore attend the meeting in question, he did not understand why you had asked me to bring the said documents to him. Eventually, I gave the documents to Mr.

LEKENE of the Chancellery who promised to take them to the meeting in question, in case the case came up for discussion. The case did not, however, come up for discussion, as I was informed the next day.

On Wednesday, 26th November 1986, I again saw the Vice Chancellor and when he asked me if, in the meantime, I had been engaged to teach part-time, I informed him that the Head of the Philosophy Department had told me that, but for the Dean's disapproval, he had wanted me to teach Epistemology on a part-time basis in the interim. As the Dean was not on seat at that moment, the Vice Chancellor summoned the Vice-Dean and, in my presence, instructed him to arrange, in conjunc-tion with the Head of the Philosophy Department that I be engaged to teach on a part-time basis pending a final determination of my case. The Vice-Dean fixed an appointment with me for the next day but, when I got there, he regretted that he had not yet seen the Head of Philosophy and that, once he had seen him, everything would be arranged and I would be informed accordingly.

On Saturday, December 13th, however, the Head of the Philosophy Depart-ment told me that, since all the courses had been allocated, it was no longer possible to assign a course for me to teach. Instead, he pledged to follow up my substantive case for recruitment with more vigour and determination.

Qualification and Competence

Sir, I have not related the above details to bore you but to give the necessary background to and accurately situate what follows.

I have now been made to understand that the reason the University commis-sion did not recruit me was because the Faculty recruitment committee had cast doubts on my qualifications and equivocated on my competence. I understand that it was argued at the Faculty committee that my publications were not in my area ofspecialization and that my Ph.D. thesis was not "deep enough" and dealt only with secondary aspects of Epistemology. It therefore, behoves me to state the following facts which are amply evident from the documentation I have already supplied to the University, in the cause of intellectual honesty and academic objectivity:

(1) I have had my intellectual formation and professional training in three of the topmost African Universities:

The University of Nigeria, Nsukka, the University of Ife, Ile-Ife, and the University of Ibadan, Ibadan. In all of these institutions I was adjudged a most outstanding student to the extent that several Universities solicited my services.

I enclose documentary evidence of the last point in the form of two letters, one from the Dean of Humanities, University of Port Harcourt, and the other from the Registrar of Obafemi Awolowo University, Ado-Ekiti.

(2) The University of Ife, on whose teaching staff I served from April 1978 to October 1986, is generally acknowledged as having the most dynamic and vibrant Philosophy Department on the entire African continent, with one of the largest stu-dent enrolments in the whole world. This reputation was greatly reinforced during the last quinquanial World Congress of Philosophy in Montreal, Canada, in 1983, where, of all African Universities, only the Department of Philosophy, University of Ife, fielded up to six members of its staff whose papers, ranging over a whole spec-trum of philosophical problem areas, were accepted to be read before the World Congress. And. as you are or should be aware, Sir, I was one of those who read a paper before that prestigious world body, - the ultimate ambition of any philosopher.

(3) My specialization for my doctoral work is in the areas of Epistemology and Metaphysics (M&E)- core areas of philosophy whose centrality and importance within the discipline is only equalled by logic which can be considered as the "soul" of philosophy. My Ph.D. thesis: *Karl Popper's Theory of Indeterminism,* was as-sessed by and defended before a jury of six *specialists* in Epistemology and Meta-physics, including an external examiner from a British University. Details of the assessment of my thesis and my performance at the Viva can easily be obtained by you or any other accredited official of the University from the Dean or Secretary of the Postgraduate School. University of Ibadan, on request. Nobody

who knows any-thing about the problems that have pre-occupied epistemologists and metaphysi-cians in recent years could possibly dismiss my Ph. D. thesis as "not deep enough" or as not making an original contribution to knowledge in that area of study.

(4) Thanks to my training and over 8 years' teaching experience in a Uni-versity which lays great emphasis on the inter-disciplinary approach in its programmes, I also have competence in teaching courses outside of my field of doctoral specializa-tion such as Social-Political Philosophy, Philosophy of Education and Medical Eth-ics.

(5) Publishing in areas outside one's specialization within the discipline is usually considered, in all Universities I know, a mark of great competence. I, therefore, cannot understand how the purported fact, even if it were true, that none of my publications is in my area of specialization could be used as a point against my suitability for recruitment. It is, moreover, not at all true that none of my publications are in my field of specialization. There are epistemological and metaphysical aspects to most of my published papers. Furthermore, my paper: "Jean-Paul Sartre on Free-dom and Responsibility," accepted for publication in *KIABARA,* directly treats an aspect of the main problem on which my Ph.D. thesis is centred. Again, my paper: 'For and Against God: a Consideration of some Traditional Arguments on the Ques-tion of God" read before the 17th World Congress of Philosophy in Montreal, Canada, in August 1983, and which will be coming out with the *Proceedings of the Congress* this year, is a direct application of the Popperian Epistemological Methodology un-derlying my Ph.D. thesis. I might also mention that I have recently finished work on a manuscript for a book: "Popperian Solutions to Some Central Philosophical Prob-lems" worked out of my Ph. D. thesis and intended as a critical expository introduc-tory text for University Students and as a didactical spring-board for philosophy-teachers.

(6) I find it somehow amusing but otherwise quite hard to understand, how I can now be adjudged incompetent to teach a course which I have taught not only competently but commendably for several years at the University of Ife.

Sir, I know that the University reserves the ultimate prerogative of recruiting into its services whoever it pleases. And, for all I know, there might be other secret criteria for eligibility in addition to the publicized ones. However, considering only the publicized criteria, I consider the rejection of my candidature both unjustifiable and unfair and hereby appeal for a reappraisal of my case.

Yours sincerely,

Godfrey B. TANGWA

CC: The Chancellor
The Vice Chancellor

Note

1. This letter is a surviving record from the period of my passage through the needle's eye into the teaching staff of The University of Yaounde, Cameroon.

5

Fonlon's Socratic Life: Its Relevance to our Political Culture and Contemporary Situation[1]

The parallels between the life of Bernard Fonlon and that of the ancient Greek philosopher, Socrates, are so striking as to make a description of the former as "Socrates in Cameroon" both legitimate and appropriate.

The respects in which Socrates towered like a colossus above his contemporaries and for which he has gained "immortality" in the annals of intellectual history are the very same respects in which Fonlon towered like a colossus above all of us, contemporary Cameroonians. Among the most important of these parallels are the following: moral integrity, intellectual courage, concern with moral perfection as the summum bonum, role as gadfly to society, use of the Maieutic art and the identification of virtue with knowledge. It is no accident that many of Fonlon's writings are replete with references to Socrates. For Fonlon, Socrates evidently served as a model that he successfully replicated.

Philosophy, they say, begins in wonder and curiosity. And what the earliest philosophers, beginning with Thales of Miletus in the western tradition, wondered and were curious about was the physical universe surrounding humans. It was Socrates who turned the focus of philosophical speculation from the mendacities of the early philosophers to speculation about man himself. "Man know Thyself" became with Socrates a procedural maxim, for he rightly saw in man a microcosm no less complex and interesting than the macrocosmic physical universe that fascinated the other philosophers. Socrates, according to the testimony of Xenophon, only discussed human concerns – what makes men good as individuals or as citizens. Knowledge in this area was, for him, the condition of a free and noble character; ignorance left a man no better than a slave.

The pre-Socratic philosophers had expended all their intellectual energy-speculating and disagreeing about the origin of the universe. Thales, for example, had postulated water as the substance of the universe, while Anaximander argued for the *apeiron,* an indeterminate undifferentiated primal mass, and Anaximenes, after careful observation of the processes of rarefaction and condensation, had settled for aer (air).

For Socrates, this type of theorizing was useless because it was too far removed from what seemed to him as man's chief and proper concern – knowledge of himself and of the right way to live his life. Accordingly, he sought to effect a shift from the search for beginnings to the search for a *telos* (end, purpose, goal), which coincides with a shift of interest form static external Nature to dynamic Man. For Socrates, if we cannot know the beginnings of the universe and of life in the unrecorded past, we can at least know the meaning, end and purpose of life here and now. Socrates was thus the first philosopher in the western tradition to introduce teleological considerations into Man's restless search for meaning, understanding and knowledge in the world in which he finds himself.

In his concern with man, the most important question became for Socrates, as it was for Fonlon in our own day, man's intrinsically valuable end. The answer to this question is not only clear and unequivocal but exactly univocal in both philosophers: man's *summum bonum* or the highest good – that which for man is worth seeking not merely as a means to some other end but as an end in itself – is the moral and intellectual personality of the individual. Between the three types of classes of human beings discernible in every society, namely, lovers of material gain/pleasure (philokerdeis), lovers of fame/honour (philotimoi) and lovers of wisdom/truth (philosophoi), both Socrates and Fonlon are agreed that the last is the best and only class worth striving to belong to. For both philosophers, the moral and intellectual faculties are one and the same; hence, the equation or identification of virtue with knowledge, vice with ignorance, and the attempt to inculcate virtue through calm reasoning and intellectual clarifications and catharsis.

Bernard Fonlon's remarkable moral courage and integrity shows that he was exactly like Socrates who, from all extant historical accounts, seems to have been such an extraordinary individual that he apparently never experienced what is commonly termed *akrasia,* weakness of will or backsliding in moral matters, which is the lot of most human beings, but always acted according to the dictates of his rational intellect and never did anything he believed to be wrong, not even to save his own life.

The temperament and moral disposition of the two men is strikingly similar.

I will illustrate with a few significant stories. The renowned historian of ancient philosophy, John Burnet in his book: *Greek Philosophy: Thales to Plato* (London, Macmillan, 1968, p.116) tells the following very interesting stories about Socrates.

> In 406 B.C.,... it fell to his (i.e. Socrates') lot to be a member of the Council of Five Hundred, and it so happened that it was the turn of the fifty representatives of the tribe of Antiochis, to which his deme belonged, to act as the executive committee of the Council at the time the generals were tried for failing to recover the bodies of the dead after the naval battle of the Arginoussai. The conduct of the trial showed that the democracy was getting into an ugly temper. It was proposed to judge all the generals together instead of taking the case of each separately. That was against the law, and Socrates, who presided, refused, in spite of popular clamour, to put the question to the meeting. The generals were ultimately condemned by an illegal procedure, but the action of Socrates made a deep impression and he referred to it with justifiable pride at his trial.
>
> A little later, during the illegal rule of the Thirty (Tyrants, that is) he had the opportunity of showing that he could not be intimidated by the other side either. The Thirty sent for him along with four others and gave them orders to arrest Lean of Salamis that he might be put to death. The four others carried out the order, but Socrates simply went home. Plato makes him say that he would probably have suffered for this if the Thirty had not been overthrown shortly after.

Now listen to the following stories told by Bernard Fonlon himself, *inter_alia*, in his paper: "'Res Una Republica" (*ABBIA: Cameroon Cultural Review*, Nos. 38-39-40, May 1982, pp. 28-29).

I know the case of a Minister who, with the heft of a heavy hand crushed an innocent *planton*. The investigating police found no guilt. LABOUR advised the Minister to reconcile with his *planton*. But the Minister got him arrested a second time. I stepped in and had him released. The case went to court, but up to now the court has not done its duty.

A high ranking man coveted the wife of a man in the street. He could have won her from him by his rank and fashion and wealth. But no. He concocted a charge of subversion against the poor man and had him kept in jail for seven years! The matter came to my notice and I had him released forthwith...

Character assassination is a common practice. I had to deal with a hail of these levelled against my co-workers. But I will just mention once (sic) which was remarkable for its puerility. At one time reports came pouring into the Ministry of Transport, Post and Telecommunications when I was in charge of it: "Total insecurity at Yaounde Airport" shrieked the headlines. A commission of the OAU was due to meet at Niamey. And the orchestrated reports said that the civil Aviation men had comploted with the captain of the Caravel to fly the President over Biafra and fly so low that the Biafrans should bring him down. At first, I dismissed all this as so much childish nonsense. But on second thought, I set up a commission of Aviation men, pilots, engineers, civil, military, white, black and carried a thorough investigation into the matter. It turned out from unquestionable evidence that, from Yaounde, the President flew over Foumban, Markurdi, Bida, to Niamey, and that, at a height of 31.000 ft, twice the height of Mount Cameroon. Where was Biafra? Far down below his route. And we spent a hefty sum in this exercise, the result of either childish stupidity or over - zealousness, or inept sheer mindless malice. This sort of thing has rampant currency in Cameroon. It is sad that so much time and energy is spent, not in constructive effort but in destructive wickedness.

It is clearly evident that it is the same thirst for justice, honesty and moral integrity that inspired the actions and reactions of both Socrates and Fonlon in the above stories.

Our contemporary situation, no less than the situation in which Socrates lived, is characterised by noisy profession and empty sloganeering about morality. But in Socrates and Fonlon we have two rare paradigms of the perfect coincidence of profession, conviction and practice. In a situation where many so-called technocrats, holding high public offices, have proved to be nothing but kleptocrats, Bernard Fonlon has shown all of us that it is possible to hold high office without abuse and corruption, that it is possible to hold high office and remain human and humble. This, I believe, is his 'immortal' contribution to our political culture and contemporary history'. Exactly like Socrates, Fonlon believed and lived up to the belief that the only thing in life worth caring for is not wealth or power or social distinction but the soul or the moral and intellectual personality. Fonlon's intellectual courage was such that he, again like Socrates, was a constant 'gadfly' in society against apathetic somnolence, the sanctification of mediocrity and the canonization of a cowardly conspiracy of silence.

As for the Socratic art, the *maieutic* "art of the midwife" to which Socrates, through a dialectical methodology sought to bring to birth and fruition the ideas conceived and nurtured in other people's minds, there are a legion of Fonlon's students who bear eloquent testimony to the healthy intellectual babies conceived, nurtured and delivered through his intellectual midwifery. Nor is his skill as an intellectual midwife lost to those who have never been privileged to sit at his feet. The man was first and foremost a teacher and all his writings are thoroughly suffused with that didactical spirit reminiscent of the Sermon on the Mount. It is a very fortunate thing for the academic and intellectual community that Fonlon finished writing his *Memoirs* before his death. It is, without any shred of doubt, the duty of the Bernard Fonlon Society (B.F.S.) to place Fonlon's *Memoirs* in printed form at the disposal of the intellectual community- as soon as possible.

We are aware of two "'worlds" in our experience: the physical or material world and the psychic or mental world. The relationship between body and mind may be philosophically problematic but no one can seriously question the existence of both the physical and the mental. Whether the mind (soul) survives the death of the body or perishes with the body at death, is a matter of dispute which remains philosophically inconclusive either way. But to these two problematic worlds must be added a third - the world of theoretical entities and systems, the world of ideas, ideals, the world of moral and intellectual exemplars. It is Karl Popper who has argued very persuasively for not only the existence but also the distinctness, independence, objectivity, autonomy and transcendence of this third world vis-à-vis the world of physical objects and the world of consciousness or mental states. He illustrates this with two "Thought experiments" (See Karl R. Popper, *Objective Knowledge: An Evolutionary Approach.* Oxford, The Clarendon Press, 1972, pp. 107-108). In the first "experiment" we are called upon to consider a situation where:

> All our machines and tools are destroyed and all our subjective learning, including our subjective knowledge of machines and tools, and how to use them. But libraries and *our capacity to learn from them survive.*

The evident result of this "experiment" is that "after much suffering, our world may get going again." In the second experiment, we are to imagine a similar situation as in the first experiment but with the crucial difference that this time all our libraries are also destroyed, so that our capacity to learn from books becomes useless. The result here, Popper believes, is that "there will be no re-emergence of our civilisation for many millennia." Careful consideration of these two experiments, Popper urges, should render clear the importance, significance and degree of autonomy of the third world as well as its cybernetic relationship with the other two worlds, especially the second world of human consciousness. Unlike the physical world which, some say, was created and will be annihilated, while others say can neither be created nor destroyed, and unlike the world of human consciousness which some say survives the death of the body while others say perishes with the body, this third world is indisputably created by human thought and artistic, moral and intellectual endeavours; but it is clearly indestructible. For what has been thought cannot be unthought.

And so it is that, while Bernard Fonlon's body today lies amouldering in the grave, his thought and ideas and ideals, like those of Socrates, go unstoppably marching on.

Note
1. Paper read during the Launching of the Bernard Fonlon Society (B.F.S.) on Thursday, Nov. 19th, 1987.

6

The Sasse Motto Fide Quaerens Intellectum[1]

The founding fathers of Sasse College, Cameroon's premier secondary pedagogical institution, chose for its motto the scholastic maxim: *fides quaerens intellectum* (faith seeking understanding), symbolized on its emblem by the mitre and the book. This is not surprising. By 1939, most institutions of higher learning, especially in EUROPE, were still under the strong influence of *scholasticism* which, within the Catholic Church, remained the unquestioned official philosophy until the early sixties when the incomparable Pope John XXIII gave the world a jolt by throwing open the ventilation of an airtight edifice to let in a breath of fresh air in his *aggiornarnento* programme which sought to bring the church out of its medieval *Weltanschauung* and keep it abreast with modem times.

Scholasticism as a philosophy may be understood as an *ensemble* of doctrines and theories elaborated in the Christian West between the 7th and 13th centuries A.D. and united by two main characteristics: a common language and methodology, on the one hand, and, on the other, submission to religious faith.

Latin was the accepted international language throughout the Christian Middle Ages and the writings of the period can further be identified by their didactic methodology which consciously avoided the oratorical mode in favour of a more direct logical approach epitomized in the Aristotelian syllogism.

Latin survived as a very important part of the curriculum in Sasse College until around 1964 when it was gently phased out. No Sasse student of my generation can easily forget someone like Father James Tol (MAHBU NGIRI! *Shocking* boy!

Shocking plus plus! Go to Tiko and sell garri!), and the zeal and competence with which he taught Latin which he evidently considered the most important subject on the curriculum, partly and quite rightly, because of its indispensability in easily grasping English grammar and syntax. The very last set of Sasse students offered Latin at the Ordinary Level London G.C.E. in 1966. I was among these last remnants of the Latinists, the others being Michael Njume, Joseph Jumbam and Christopher Chukoyo.

Using the Tolean foundation, we drudged through Virgil and Caesar's *Gallic Wars* as an extra curricular activity with the very kind help of the meticulous Father Stumpel (Fr. Küng)

Parenthetically, it must be remarked that the suppression of Latin from the curriculum, no matter what might be said in its favour, has shown its negative effect in the very poor grasp of English that is discernable even among our University graduates today. The initial suppression of the oratorical element in pedagogy also filtered from Sasse (the *primus inter pares* of our Colleges) to nearly all other secondary institutions in Anglophone Cameroon and has shown its effect, up to the present, in the paucity of literary talent and political astuteness among Cameroonian Anglophones vis-à-vis their francophone counterparts. Maybe that is controversial. In any case, the connection between sophistry, especially oratory, expediency and "success" in public life is one that has been well known since the time of Socrates through Machiavelli to the present.

Scholasticism must be credited with giving precision to the distinction between the natural and the supernatural orders, between *faith* and *reason*. At the same time, it assumed the superiority of faith over reason, the supernatural over the natural, theology over philosophy. The *fides* always came before the *intellectum* just as the mitre stands above the book in the S.J.C. emblem.

This legacy made it inevitable that priestly training would feature in the scheme of things; hence, the *Holy Family Seminary* which was part and parcel of Sasse College. Today some 23 SOBAN (Sasse Old Boys Association) priests are usually proudly listed, among them, bishops and archbishops. But this census loses sight of the fact that Bishop Rogan College, Soppo, is a direct offshoot of Sasse College and that priestly training has continued there. The scores who were "called but not chosen" must not also be forgotten, for here, like in the Olympics, there must be some credit for even merely competing. Many prominent SOBANS are ex-Seminarians.

A golden jubilee is an occasion for a certain measure of justified glamourization and positive highlighting. It should also be a time for a certain measure of self-critical stock-taking.

The underlying conception of education operative in Sasse and the other Colleges later established on the same model (notably; Q.R.C. Okoyong, Sacred Heart College, Mankon, Our Lady of Lourdes, Mankon, and even C.P.C. Bali and Saker Baptist College, Limbe) was too elitist, inevitably infusing in the students the idea of not only being very special but of being set aside. This is the idea of secondary education for the privileged select few. Gaining admission into any such institution was equivalent to passing through the needle's eye. Although in Sasse the students referred to the section where the Seminarians lived as "the monastery," the entire institution had many monastic elements: set in a jungle, entirely boarding and strictly single-sexed. It was not until the early sixties that some colleges were started which deviated from this model - notably, St. Bede's College. Ashing, and St. Augustine's College, Kumbo. In Kumbo, Fr. Nielen, who started the College, caused a country-wide "scandal" by beginning in a community hall, right in the centre of town, to which students (both boys and girls) came daily from home and by accepting corn, beans, potatoes, goats, fowls etc, from very poor parents in lieu of fees. In Sasse itself, it took the ultra radicalism of Fr. Cunningham to experiment with admitting female students into the college. The experiment was, however, short lived as His Lordship, the proprietor of the College, soon ordered a return to the *status quo ante.* It was the same Fr. Cunningham who permitted the first group of female students (as far as I know) to visit Sasse College as a troupe for a cultural activity. Recall the *Mikado* players from Okoyong who caused so much understandable excitement in Sasse in, I can't now recollect, whether it was 1964 or 1965.

The meeting point between *faith* and *reason* is holiness or moral integrity. Moral integrity is a profane or secular virtue required of all human persons without distinction and without any religious pre-condition. What Sasse College set out to do for its students, as encaptured in its motto was, therefore, not only to infuse faith and knowledge but to make of them morally upright persons. It is only this third objective, moreover, that is equally within the reach of all. We cannot all be priests and we cannot all be intellectuals. But whether priest or layman, whether religious or secular, whether geniuses or dunces, whether academic successes or failures, we can and ought to live morally upright lives. In the end, when all's said and done, and the chips are all down, this is the only thing that really counts.

On this occasion, we should salute those SOBANS in our public life who have left or are creating a legacy of moral integrity, uprightness and incorruptibility. But self-critical awareness should not permit us to gloss over those others who are subverting this legacy: people in our public life who have somehow managed to combine in their personality all the worst elements of both the Anglophone and francophone systems: people who comport themselves with a certain roguish confidence and who could sell their very mothers into slavery for a mess of pottage in the form of position, possession or whatever.

The majority of SOBANS are sons of peasants. But, to look at some of these fellows today, one could hardly, by any stretch of the imagination, link them with their peasant background. They create such forbiddingness and inaccessibility around them that even their college contemporaries approach them with fear and trembling and, in some cases, (even if they were classmates back in Sasse) dare not address them by their first name or even by name at all. It has to be *Commissaire, Capitain, Directeur, Professeur, General, Patron,* etc. It is inconceivable that some of these people could today spend even a single night in the very village where, only a few decades ago, they lived, doing nothing better than hunting rabbits and fetching firewood and water.

The demands of morality are equalitarian and absolutely uncompromising. Before these demands, our state or situation in life is irrelevant. Whether priest, religious, lay person or pagan, whether man or woman, rich or poor, intellectually gifted or not, they remain exactly the same for one and for all. There are indeed priests who out-lay lay people, making us wonder what business fellows like that really have doing anywhere near a church. They make a bold pretence of the whole thing, mourning holy rhetoric, but leading lives any pagan would be ashamed of. Such "abominations of desolation" standing in Holy Places should teach us one lesson: morality is supreme and faith must manifest itself in holiness. Hence, it cannot be deduced from the official labelling of a particular state of life as "lay" (or whatever) that those who embrace it are not called to the highest flights of sanctity.

The dictum *fides quaerens intellectum* goes back to St. Anselm (A.D. 1033-1109), Bishop of Canterbury, who is famous in intellectual history for his ontological "proof" of God's existence. Anselm's argument is simply charming in its simplicity. It is addressed as a prayer to God (since faith must precede reason) and is ostensibly calculated to convince the fool of Psalm 14 (who says in his heart: "there is no God") that he is a fool.

Anselm starts by defining God as "something a greater than which cannot be conceived" (*aliquid quo nihil maius cogitari posit*). Even the fool of Psalm 14 would understand such a definition and the concept of God is thus clearly in his understanding even though he does not understand that it exists. So, for Anselm, something-a-greater-than-which-cannot-be-conceived clearly exists in the understanding (*in intellectu*). Now, many things may exist in the understanding (i.e. *in intellectu*) which do not exist in reality (*in re*), e.g. chimeras, winged horses, centaurs, etc. But, something a greater than which cannot be conceived cannot exist *only* in the understanding (*in intellectu*). For if it did, then something greater could be conceived, namely, one that exists *both* in the understanding (*in intellectu*) and in reality (*in re*). It follows then that *something than which a greater cannot be conceived* cannot be merely conceived of without existing, for then, it would not be *that than which a greater cannot be conceived*. Hence the inescapable conclusion: God, being *that than which nothing greater can be conceived*, exists both *in intellectu* and *in re*.

This Anselmian argument looks very simple, but since its first formulation in the Middle Ages up to the present time, the best human intellects have been unable to agree regarding its soundness or unsoundness. Some have regarded it as a knock-out proof of God's existence while others have regarded it as merely a charming exercise in verbal or conceptual gymnastics. The argument has found both defenders and detractors in all ages including ours. Some detractors have even gone as far as formulating an ontological "disproof of God's existence.

On my part, I submit that the existence of God is not the kind of issue about which there could be a knock down proof or disproof. The best approach, for one who wants to limit himself within the realm of reason would seem to be to make a guess or conjecture in line with the sum-total of available evidence. But a guess or conjecture, no matter how strongly we feel certain about it, remains open to correction or revision, in the light of any further evidence. This tentativeness underlines our human limitations and imposes humility. To raise doubts about things even of which we feel certain is healthy because it guards against dangerous dogmatism and infuses both humility and tolerance. However, methodic doubting need not paralyse action or diminish commitments.

A story is told of Chuang-Chou who dreamt that he was a butterfly. When he woke from his dream, he started wondering whether perhaps he was not a butterfly, dreaming that he was a man. Even such hyperbolic doubt need not paralyse action or diminish commitments, for on the sum-total of available evidence, Chuang-Chou should easily have put his bet on the conjecture: "I am a man."

Faith may be counterposed to *reason,* but each really involves the other. For faith is not and cannot be a mere leap in the dark. It is a commitment backed by good reasons. On the other hand, given human epistemological limitations, the most self-assuring process of reasoning can only lead to a justified acceptance of what at bottom is only a conjecture.

The Sasse Motto: *Fides quaerens intellectum* is thoroughly justified. Faith indeed must seek understanding, but understanding or reason itself, in the human context, cannot rise above a justified faith.

Note

1. Written on the occasion of the Golden Jubilee of St. Joseph's College. Sasse, Buea (founded in 1939) and published in the *GOLDLN JUBILEE MAGAZINE* and in *CAMEROON Tribune* of Friday, January 27. 1989.

7

The Plight of the Ex-seminarian and Ex-religious in Modern Cameroon[1]

I should begin this essay with some preliminary confessions: I am one of these people that I am about to write about, having quit the path to the priesthood less than three years from the final destination. I have not conducted any "study" on the plight of ex-Seminarians and Religious in Cameroon. Nevertheless, I have been a very careful and impressionable observer and my own personal experience has been a subject of continuing personal reflection.

Quitting the path to the priesthood or religious life at an advanced stage can, perhaps, be compared to baling out of an airborne aircraft. Without a parachute, the action is almost certainly suicidal; with a parachute, two putative results are possible. This metaphor does not need much interpretation. The "airborne aircraft" is the accelerated journey towards the priesthood or religious life, as the case may be. By "parachute" I mean a generalised psychological disposition (preparation) to undergo a radical change in one's chosen course of life. The course of an arrow in fight cannot be easily changed.

An implicit assumption here, of course, is that the initial bid for the priesthood or religious life was made in all earnestness, honesty and sincerity. The possibility is not to be ruled out that some make the bid for lack of a better alternative at a given moment or merely as an agreeable way of passing the time while looking out for something more suitable. Sometimes too, an initially earnest bid gets subverted along the way at that point where the person in question becomes convinced that he or she should quit but continues as a matter of convenience along the line of least resistance. I remember when I quit the seminar back in 1972, one of my co-Seminarians who tried to persuade me to reconsider my decision told me:

Godfrey, at this stage, how do you think you are going to survive out there with your 0/Levels (G.C.E, Ordinary Level)? As a priest, at least you are going to be assured of a good house, a car and three good square meals a day! A genius like you, do you want to end up as a primary school teacher? Or is this celibacy thing your problem? Please, I assure you it is not that bad. The problem is only here in the Seminary. Once in the Parish, all the married ladies and young girls will be completely at your disposal. Please, think *very carefully!*"

If someone quits the path who, in the first place, should never have taken it, or who should have quit earlier but kept on out of sheer convenience, we can no longer really talk of a "change in one's chosen course of life." But given that the bid was undertaken and sustained in all seriousness, what I am saying is that, without adequate psychological preparation, abandoning the path to the priesthood or religious life at an advanced stage, is almost suicidal. "Suicidal" here is by no means to be taken as limited to the metaphorical sense. Some of the serious errors an unprepared ex-Seminarian or Religious is likely to commit in the profane world, such as rushing into an impossible marriage or trying too hard to scrub clean all traces of religious formation, can and have been, in some cases, the ultimate cause of death.

Now, what are the putative results for someone who bales out of the Seminary, Priesthood, Sisterhood or other religious life armed with a "parachute," that is, fully psychologically prepared for such a change? To continue with our metaphor, the first possibility is a faulty or unfortunate landing, resulting in fractured limbs. A "faulty landing" may result from an inability to adjust quickly enough to changing conditions or from lack of sheer technique and style. An "unfortunate landing" occurs when, in spite of technique, style and manoeuvrability, the parachutist lands on rough or hostile terrain. A "broken limb" in this metaphor translates into a disability carried throughout life such as pathological puritanism or depravity usually manifested through extremism in abstention or indulgence, respectively.

There certainly is something odd about someone who quits the path to the priesthood or religious life and ends up as a prostitute (of either sex) or as a thief, embezzler, swindler, notorious liar, etc. This oddity is not to be expressed in the form: 'How can an ex-Seminarian/Religious do such a thing?" but rather in the form: "How could such a person ever have wanted to become a Priest/Religious?"

The second possibility is a "safe landing" which translates into a balanced individual, well-adjusted in his/her present circumstances, integrating earlier ideas and experiences, lessons from earlier failures and mistakes, into the reality of present adjusted circumstances.

For this to happen, I believe that the person in question must, from the onset, have a sense of proportion and the right perspective on tillings. The most important aspect of this correct perspective is the realisation that the fact of being a human being is more important than the state of life one embraces or the material conditions of one's life. It is commonly believed that priests and religious are called to live a holier life than lay persons. In spite of the very plausible arguments that can be used to support this belief I dare say that it is totally mistaken and leads to the erroneous identification of holiness with such things as celibacy, habit wearing, church-going etc, which, in themselves, cannot and do not make any one holy. The call to holiness, in my view, is addressed equally and indiscriminately to human beings qua human beings, irrespective of their particular state in life (priestly, lay, religious or pagan), no matter their particularizing circumstances (male, female, rich, poor, learned, unlearned, etc). This point of view would, no doubt, be considered as *heretical* by some people but I am persuaded of its correctness, and would have attempted substantiating it in more detail if I had more space at my disposal.

All I have said so far, if at all plausible, is valid rather generally and you may already be complaining that I have not addressed myself to my topic. What then, in addition to the above, can be said about the plight of the ex-Seminarian or Religious in present day Cameroon, particularly?

The path to the priesthood/religious life is circumscribed by certain moral/spiritual values. One of the most important problems, then, that faces someone in present day Cameroon who has been oriented to appreciate those values and, in fact, to consider them as superior to all other values, is the sheer materialism of the society. Cameroon Society is exaggeratedly materialistic. The only things which are greatly prized in our society are material possessions: money, wives, houses, children, cars, clothes, food, drinks, etc. To be destitute of these things in Cameroon is to place yourself in a position where nobody respects you or even notices that you exist.

I lived a good part of my adult life in Nigeria and used to think that Nigerian society was irredeemably materialistic; until I came back to Cameroon. Looking back from here, I must confess that Nigerians revere certain non-material values which nobody seems to recognise in Cameroon: such things as learning for its own sake, incorruptibility, personally perilous pursuit of truth and justice, etc. That is why, in Nigeria, people like Tai Solarin, Chinua Achebe, Gani Fawehimi, Wole Soyinka, etc, are national heroes in spite of their very visible lack of material possessions. These are people no one can bribe or bully to abandon their principles/convictions.

Tai is well identified with his khaki shorts and, while he was still principal of his famous Mayflower College, Ikenny, visitors to the school frequently mistook him for the compound cleaner. For over eight years I taught in the same faculty with Wole Soyinka at the University of Ife. Never once did I see him wear a western suit. He was always in T-shirt and trousers and occasionally in *danshiki*. In fact, he received his Nobel award for Literature in 1986 wearing a simple *danshiki*. Even now, as a world celebrity, he does not mind anybody addressing him simply as "Wole."

But here in Cameroon, I find that even my secondary school contemporaries who have "made it" want to be approached with bended knees and addressed "properly." The best Cameroonian pure scientist known to me, the only one so far listed in the WHO'S WHO IN THE WORLD IN CHEMISTRY, was once, not so long ago, pushed out of the Vice Chancellor's office right here at the University of Yaounde because he had the temerity of going to see the mortal god dressed in his laboratory overcoat. At least that would never have happened anywhere in Nigeria.

An ex-Seminarian or Religious in Cameroon finds him/herself greatly pressurised to get married, breed children, buy plots, build houses, count his/her material blessings with appropriate ceremonies and celebrations at appropriate times, and distribute largesse to all and sundry. Failure to do any of these things will earn him/her the title "queer" or "mad." He/she would be laughed at openly wherever people gather together: bars, churches, *njangi* houses, etc. Now, nobody can easily live in a society where he/she is consistently considered as a crank or some other sort of oddity.

Another problem that faces an ex-Seminarian/Religious in Cameroon is that he/she suddenly finds him/herself as a highly qualified but uncertificated adult applicant in a job market where the greatest assets are youth and certificates – those at any rate arbitrarily approved by the powers – that – be.

Today, unlike in the past, an ex-Seminarian, say, would usually have some diploma in Philosophy or Theology to show for his years of study which would usually have covered a much wider spectrum of disciplines. To apply for employment in the Public Service he would first be required to compile a "dossier" submitting his diploma for evaluation and "equivalence." With some luck, this exercise may take about three years. Meanwhile, his age would have inevitably attained the 35 year limit beyond which, for some unfathomable reason, no one can be offered employment in the Cameroon Public Service. Two options are now open: with the help of all the corrupt public officers populating our public institutions, he might falsify his age and other personal documents appropriately or he might try the private sector. The Catholic Educational Service would be the most likely choice. But there the rudest shock would await him. The Catholic Educational Authorities do not recognise his degree obtained from the Catholic Major Seminary for purposes of employment! At this stage he may go on his knees begging to be employed on the basis of his Advanced Levels (A/Levels) or Ordinary Levels (O/Levels) but, of course, the Education Secretary would kindly and patiently explain that what he needs is a "trained teacher." It is now time for our ex-Seminarian to contemplate suicide or else boldly return to his village to live the life of a subsistence peasant farmer.

Note

1. Written at the request of sister Mercy Hongan, editor of the Catholic monthly *CAMEROON PANORAMA,* this paper was published in No. 319 of that magazine in January *1991.*

8

Bernard Fonlon Evening Monday 19th November 1990[1]

I have greatly enjoyed all the lectures given this evening. I have learnt a lot of things I didn't know before. All the lectures have raised several questions in my mind. However, I'll refrain from asking any questions and limit myself to the following brief comment.

Many thinkers have thought that there must be one single overpowering motive or principle underlying all human striving, actions and reactions. It is in this way that Karl Marx identified *wealth* or the economic mode of the individual's existence as the key to all social dynamics while Sigmund Freud identified it as *sex*, that is, repressed and usually unconscious sexual drives. But, I think both Marx and Freud were wrong. My own suggestion would be that the key to all human actions is to be found in the concept of *power* considered in its most generic signification. I believe with Bertrand Russell that love of power in the generic sense, just like lust, is such a strong motive that it influences most people's actions more than they think.

Now, if we limit ourselves to political power, it is easy to see why it is imperative that power should be tamed. It has often been remarked that power tends to corrupt and that absolute power corrupts absolutely. What is not so often pointed out is that power is delightful and that absolute power must be absolutely delightful. It is the extreme delightfulness of power taken together with its corruptive tendency that imposes, even from a common-sensical point of view, the imperative to tame power. What is at stake is our collective survival and well-being.

In the struggle to tame power, there are two moral duties, one from the point of view of those who wield power, the other from the point of view of those under power. Incidentally, the moral duties I have in mind are ones which Bernard Fonlon abundantly exemplified in his life.

The first of these, from the point of view of those in power, is humility, the humility to take criticism, even to seek it, as the only way not only to avoid preventable blunders but also for general progressive improvement. Fonlon was a perfectionist; and yet, as one of the young men who used to live with him told me recently, he was always very happy when anybody criticized him. Sometimes, according to this witness, he used to have a long heated argument with his master over some historical detail or some small point of grammar such as the use of a word, punctuation mark or correct spelling. They would consult the most compelling authorities and whenever he was proved right, Fonlon would raise his hands to his head in contrite defeat and immediately give him a handsome reward. Contrast that with the attitude of one of my colleagues at the University who recently, in my presence, told a student who had come to his office to argue some point made by the former in the course of a class lecture: *Ecoutez, Monsieur, un étudiant n 'est pas un professeur, eh! Sortez d'ici!* One of the indispensable *prolegomena* to democracy in our country would, no doubt, be a re-orientation of the educational system in which most of those we flatter with the appellation "Leaders of Tomorrow" are formed.

God created man with two eyes but unfortunately placed both on the same side of the head, instead of more wisely placing one each on opposite sides. The consequence of this "divine mistake" is that no human being (including, it needs saying, those in power), no matter how gifted or talented, can see any issue from more than a single point of view. And yet there are infinite points of view for any given issue. People who seek criticism greatly fortify themselves against violent surprises along the path of human fallibility. To ride on the wings of one man's wisdom is to choose the ditch for our destination.

From the point of view of those under power/authority, what is required is the virtue of *honesty* and the *courage* to back it up. Richard Joseph in his book: *Gaullist Africa: Cameroon Under Ahmadou Ahidjo*, has witnessed how during cabinet meetings when the president had delivered some powerful and far-reaching policy Speech, total silence would descend on the hall, no one daring to contradict or even comment in any other way on what the *Leviathan* had said. Very often it was only Bernard Fonlon who would have the temerity to raise his hand, clear his throat, and launch into a critique of what the president had just said.

This culture of silence has permeated all facets of our national life. Sometimes while teaching at the University, I would purposely say something glaringly false or shockingly stupid, expecting my students to immediately rise up like one person in protest. But, more often than not, I would find them nodding their heads like foolish wise men until I assure them that what I had said was false or stupid and then they would nod again like wise fools.

When this culture of silence has been broken, it has usually been to concur and applaud. Even the most brilliant among our Ministers often preface everything they say in public with the refrain: "As his Excellency, the Head of State has said..." Well, may be that is quite understandable. But I also find that even during purely scientific discussions, when the *president de séance or president du jury* has spoken, every subsequent speaker is very careful not to contradict him but only to support what was already in his omniscient speech even if unexpressed. When the Catholic Bishops published their now famous pastoral letter in March, the official media first ignored it completely, then praised it exaggeratedly as being exactly what His Excellency the Head of State had been saying all the time, before ignoring it again.

I believe that adults should have the courage always to honestly say what they truly think about issues especially those which affect their lives directly. It is even a joy to suffer for what one truly and strongly believes. Power tends to turn those wielding it into mortal gods and, if those under their power keep silent for fear of suffering the inconveniences of expressing unpalatable views, those in power inevitably assume divine attributes, except benevolence, of course.

An adult should never allow him/herself to be made to "eat shit" in silence without protesting. If she/he does, she/he should never ever complain. Many Cameroonians have been suffering in silence for too long. From this view-point, it is quite true that we have the government we deserve.

Note

1.   Comment made "from the floor" during the 4th Bernard Fonlon Evening (Monday, Nov. 19fh, 1990), after lectures by Sindjoun Pokam, Lovette Eiango, Verkijika Fanso. Jean-Baptiste Sipa, Paddy Mbawa and Kange Ewane, under the general theme: "THE IMPLICATIONS OF DEMOCRACY IN CAMEROON." While making my free comment I noticed that the audience was listening keenly and not showing any signs of impatience or boredom. So I took liberties and spoke at length. Afterwards the officials of the B.F.S. told me it was a very interesting comment and could I put it down in writing to be published with the papers? I did, although the lectures of that remarkable evening have never, up till today, been published.

9

Fale Wache, Lament of a Mother[1]

In this poem, Wache, taking refuge behind a woman whose son, Ndikochong, has gone overseas and refused to return, lays bare the festering wounds of our contemporary socio-political-economic situation and stops short only of rubbing caustic acid on them. Wache describes, diagnoses, with razor sharpness but refrains from prescribing. The poem is in the form of enthymemic or truncated arguments whose missing components are not far to fetch if one wanted to proceed by the method of uncompromising Aristotelian syllogisms. The missing links can be supplied variously from Soyinka, Armah, Cabral, Fanon, etc. The whole poem is an outpouring of long repressed or suppressed sentiments.

Of course, Ndikochong is not overseas, or rather, the overseas where he is, is right here in Cameroon! Ndikochong is that Cameroonian with a foothold within the ruling class, who is not actually in power but nonetheless, has the power of being close to power; he is in the corridors of power. Ndikochong is that Cameroonian who has sold his own people for the price of continuing to enjoy the crumbs failing from his masters' table. When he completes that betrayal, he might even be called up to feed from the table. He will do this by whispering to his masters that he knows all trouble-makers in his village and their diabolical plans and schemes. He would be most convincing when he "reveals" that his own mother is not only one of them but their ring-leader.

Soon, a "security- report" originating from Ndikochong himself would allege that the people of his village are amassing arms from some neighbouring country to destabilise the state. Whereupon, an entire company of the National Army would descend on the tiny village, at 3.000 a.m., breaking doors, beating up sleepers, looting and raping, and ordering everyone, in their loincloths, '*dentité*' in hand, to assemble and sit on the bare ground in the central village square.

Nothing, of course, would be found except farming implements, a few dane guns and blunt machetes. The soldiers would withdraw after twenty-four hours, without apologies, without even an explanation for this brutal rape of an innocent village. But Ndikochong would pluck his plums. His loyalty to the regime would now be considered beyond a shred of doubt. He would be rewarded with a Pajero to enable him visit his "constituency" regularly in spite of the impossible condition of the roads and keep an eye on the traditional stool on which he now intends to sit, once the recalcitrant illiterate now occupying it is "taken care of." This time around, Ndikochong's name would surely be on the long list of those accompanying the big man himself on his next regular "private visit" abroad. It is while popping *Pom Perignons* there that his mother would die from the effect of the severe beating she received the night the soldiers came and Ndikochong would return to receive the terse message: THE WOMAN DIED.

For the hard-of-hearing, we might even say it is plainer language. The colonial masters with all their *dominus vobiscums, pater nosters, mea culpas and kyrie eleisons* did us little harm, really. Under their regime did we not enjoy fairly good roads and market our cash crops fairly profitably? Now that they are gone, their thrones are not empty but occupied by our own *'shons'* of the *'shoil,'* black white men who have proved to be not only better exploiters and oppressors but also inconscient looters of the National Treasury and public property. The line is between oppressors and oppressed, rapers and raped, robbers and robbed, wrong doers and the wronged.

Note
1. Written on the occasion of the launching of Francis Wache's book, a long poem entitled *Lament of a Mother,* in 1991.

10

On The Television Programme "The Debate"[1]

The Producer
"The Debate,"
C.R.T.V, Yaounde.

I have what I might describe as *serious reservations* concerning the T.V. programme "The Debate." Let me try to put my points simply and clearly.

All those involved in the production and presentation of this programme are evidently very talented and gifted persons. But these facilities are mostly wasted on this programme. The programme is no doubt *entertaining*. But a programme of this type ought to be more than just that. It is also a *silly* programme. But if it were only silly and entertaining it would be harmless even if useless. However, it also happens to be a *dangerous* programme.

Let me try to unpack these loaded statements. Purely formal debates (in which the views expressed are not to be equated with the true opinion of the person expressing them) unquestionably have a great didactic value especially at secondary school level where pupils learn the techniques of reasoning, argumentation, self-expression, self-confidence, etc. For such formal debates it is usually advisable to choose harmless topics such as:

- Which is sweeter, foofoo corn or achuu?
- Which is better, to be a man or a woman?
- Between a mountain and a valley, which would you choose?
- Is it better to be too tall or too short?
- If your father and mother are drowning, who will you save first?
- When you go to heaven, will you prefer to sit on God's right hand or left?
- Would you prefer a trip to the moon or to mars?
- Boys are finer than girls.
- A donkey is better than a horse.
- Witches exist.

One doesn't expect normal adults to engage in debates of such topics. Adults should debate more substantive issues. But if adults are to engage in debate of more substantive issues then a very strong reason is needed if this is to be done in a purely formal manner, that is, if they are to debate as a merely intellectual exercise whose results are not to be considered as representing reality or as providing guides for action or conduct. The reason here is that the views expressed regarding such substantive issues could mislead a lot of people who have no time to ponder the issues for themselves. This danger increases several times over if the debate is carried over the mass media as is the case with "The Debate." Examples of what I have termed substantive issues are the following:

- Is Abortion right or wrong?
- Is Euthanasia justifiable?
- Should contraceptives be made available to teenagers?
- Is Capital punishment right?
- Which is better, polygamy or monogamy? ,
- Should husbands and wives operate joint bank accounts?
- Which is better, democracy or dictatorship?
- Should traditional medicine be encouraged?
- Is Artificial Insemination right or wrong?
- Should bride price be proscribed?

To ask people who are not only adults but intellectuals to debate such issues publicly is to predispose the viewers to be expecting to learn something or, at least, to be enlightened. Now, if the debaters then proceed to debate such issues with all show of seriousness, as is the case in "'The Debate," and a panel of judges even declares one side winner, then the reminder that the views expressed are not the true views of those expressing them, is neither here nor there. If "The Debate," were a drama programme one would understand; but if it were, the explanation that the views expressed are not those of the various actors would be quite unnecessary. But, in fact, "the Debate" cannot pass for a programme of comic drama even though there is a lot of clowning in it. The issues involved are simply too weighty to be handled in this sort of trifling manner.

As a matter of fact, most of the arguments used in the programme have been either fallacious or sophistical. In purely formal debates, sophistical and fallacious arguments are always very efficacious because of their strong psychological appeal. But in substantive debates they signal the untenability of the views or positions they are supposed to support. When two brilliant jurists of the calibre of Dr. Ngwafor and Dr. Anyangwe appear regularly on such a programme, vividly expressing phantom arguments which one might applaud in adolescent children, it must be said that they are selling themselves far below their market value. And if, there be nothing wrong with that, they are, at any rate, likely to lead large numbers of credulous people seriously astray.

My suggestion: **The programme** "the Debate" should continue to treat substantive issues but not in a trivial manner. The issues should be debated seriously and frankly. People should express well-considered or *informed* views, views they are convinced about, views on which they can stake their learning and reputation. This means inter-alia, that the producer of the programme would have to go out and seek people who are well informed on the particular issue being debated and who *would* take positions out of conviction and not for the mere purpose of making a show. In such an arrangement the moderator of the debate would often have to play the *advocatus diaboli* to force the debaters to clarify their positions satisfactorily and that is understandable.

With this type of arrangement the debaters would be constantly changing according to the issues instead of the present quasi-permanent arrangement, which to a sensitive regular viewer, must already be comparable to two familiar differently pitched cymbals clanging.

If the Programme must remain exactly as it is in format, then the best thing would be to limit the issues debated to the sort of trivial topics of which I have given some examples in paragraph three above. That way; it would, of course, be a waste of precious air time but most other programmes so far are exactly that any way.

If neither of the above two options can be adopted, then a third alternative is to limit the programme to secondary school children who would thereby not only be able to amuse themselves thoroughly but would actually profit from the exercise in the ways already specified.

I have not expressed the above views as a purely academic exercise. They are my well-considered views expressed in all seriousness. I am, of course, ready to modify or change them if offered convincing arguments for doing so. In other words, my views are open to debate but not, of course, to purely formal debate.

Note

1. Written on 23/12/90 and delivered by hand to the addressee, this piece was subsequently published in *Le Messager* (English edition). No. 024 of Thursday, April 25, 1991.

11

Is There Really an Anglophone Problem in Cameroon?[1]

If there is an "Anglophone problem" in this country, what exactly is the problem? If there is no Anglophone problem, then what the hell is the problem with Anglophones? What are they always complaining about? So whichever way you look at it, there is a problem even if it turns out to be the problem of assuming wrongly that there is a problem where there is none.

Now, is there one problem or a catalogue of problems? It would be unwise to assume that there is only one single underlying problem as it would be to assume that there is a plethora of unrelated problems. Only careful observation, description, analysis and reflection can clarify the issue.

A people's identity is very much tied to their history. If we throw a historical bird's eye view on our recent history we can see that we have evolved within the last 30 years from "The Bilingual United Republic of Cameroon" to "The Republic of Cameroon."

The sign-posts along that historical path include the Foumban Constitutional Conference (1960), Referendum and Reunification (1961), Single Party Rule (1966), Unitary State (1972), New Deal Regime (1982), Return to Multiparty Politics (1990).

Whatever positive elements there may be in this evolution, it is incontrovertible that today many Anglophones feel like a conquered people. Evidence of a completely abandoned area strikes one from Kumba through Mamfe to Nkambe, a journey that, in colonial days, could be done in three days but which today cannot be done in six days without a lot of good luck.

What has happened, generally, I believe, is that, beginning with the Foumban Conference, Anglophones have gradually lost their bargaining power, as an identifiable group of people with a common history/destiny, shared values, aims, objectives and way of thinking. This loss of bargaining power is directly connected with the lack of a credible leadership, exacerbated by the inability or failure of the rank and file to stand up for their rights or take their destiny firmly in hand.

I shall try to illustrate the above claims with examples. All the examples I shall use are true stories although they may not be entirely free from apocryphal elements. Those referred to in these stories, who are very well known and who know themselves equally well, are encouraged to respond to these stories so as to confirm or disconfirm the apocryphal elements, if any.

The primary school teachers turned politicians who led Anglophones into Reunification were conceptually ill-equipped to negotiate fair terms for the union. No one should blame them, as it was a matter of invincible ignorance. There is no doubt that the overwhelming choice of reunification at the 1961 referendum was a consciously genuine, fair and right choice on the part of the Anglophone masses, out of the choices presented I believe that, if the referendum were reconducted today, with the same options, the outcome would be the same. Those who think that the "Anglophone problem" is a problem of secession are completely mistaken. Those who talk about "Ambazonia" are an eccentric minority. Not that their case lacks coherence, but rather that, up till now, there has really been nothing of sufficient gravity to make it generally persuasive.

The problems that there are have been mainly procedural problems which should have been squarely addressed and solved or resolved progressively as and when they arose in the light of practical experience and a better conceptual grasp of the situation.

The Foumban agreement, for instance, in spite of having been a raw deal for Anglophones, was a deal all the same. Now, instead of correcting the situation as and when the opportunities came, Anglophones allowed it to degenerate from a raw-deal into a no-deal situation. The Foumban deal, for example, did provide for bi-culturalism, bilingualism, relative autonomy and juridic equality such as in the provision that the President and Vice President of the Republic could not come from one and the same federated state.

But by 1972, all these guarantees, in spite of the efforts of people like Augustine Jua and Bernard Fonlon, had been unilaterally abrogated in actual practice. If Dr. Foncha's dramatic resignation had occurred about that time, things might have been salvaged. Unfortunately, it came two decades too late. And let no one put all the blame on Foncha. All other Anglophones in positions of power/

70

responsibility did no better. What is true is that many of them suddenly found themselves in personally incredibly lucrative positions. But even those who were forced to "eat shit" did so in humble silence in the hope perhaps that their zombiism would sooner or later earn them desired rewards.

Now the illustrative stories. A story is told of an Anglophone whom President Ahidjo once summoned from the province to Yaounde. Scared out of his wits, he pondered what crime he might have unwittingly committed and came to the conclusion that it must be connected with certain things he had recently written and had published. So he gathered all his publications, carefully planned and rehearsed how to demonstrate that, in spite of appearances, all he had written was ultimately in support of His Excellency, and set out for Yaounde. In Yaounde, he stayed with his "countryman," a minister, and they together carefully discussed what he should answer to several questions which they imagined he might be asked. He reported at the Presidency the next day and was ushered in before the awesome presence of Ahidjo. "Na you bex?," asked Ahidjo. Our man got up and bowed until his forehead touched the floor before answering "Yes, your Almighty".

"You fit keep secret?," came the next question. Again, our man bowed until his head touched the floor before answering that he was the greatest secrets keeper on earth.

Ahidjo then smiled and announced: "I wan put you for my government. I wan make you ministre." This time, our man prostrated full length, Yoruba-style, before the Leviathan.

When he got up, Ahidjo whispered conspiratorially that this was still a secret between the two of them and that he should not breathe a word of it to anybody.

Our man came out feeling like someone who had been instantly transformed into a minor deity. He felt as if he could fly. But as he quickened his springy steps, a problem suddenly occurred to him. What would he say when he got back to his countryman, the minister, whose job Ahidjo had just transferred to him with a warning not to tell anybody yet? He found himself in a big dilemma. So, instead of going directly back to his friend's house, he went into some obscure off-license. Meanwhile, back in his countryman's house, anxiety over his safety slowly rose to fever pitch. As darkness started descending over Yaounde, his countryman could no longer contain his alarm at home and went out to try to find out what might have transpired. Experience decided him to first check discreetly at the maximum security prison, BMM Kondengui. It is while he was there that our man, under cover of darkness, quickly sneaked into his house, took his bag and left immediately for the province without as much as leaving a word for his countryman, the ex-minister soon-to-be. Now, do you think someone who comes into power in this way would care one shit about his people or anyone else?

Another Anglophone who rose to hold one of the most powerful posts in the country was first spotted by the regime as a good double agent while he was still a student. Graduated, he was called to higher duties and functions. Ahidjo used to put millions of francs at his disposal to go and do "intelligence work" in his own province. When he returned, he would write reports and recommendations. In one of his reports he had "discovered" that his own people were not sincere militants of the CNU and that the Fons of the North West Province were too powerful and, for that reason, constituted a serious security risk to the regime. He recommended that the regime should find every possible means to subvert and reduce the power and influence of the Fons over their people.

The attempt to marginalise the Anglophone heritage, so as to eventually simply wipe it out has been systematic. But the real tragedy is that it is individual

Anglophones who have usually been co-opted to carry out this project. This Anglophobia can be seen in both simple actions such as that of changing, by decree, the name of a town from ""Victoria" to "Limbe" and in more weighty ones such as the attempt to abolish the entire Anglophone educational system, which was attempted in 1984 under guise of reforms. An Anglophone minister was again charged with this task which, but for the vigilance of some Anglophone teenagers, would have been accomplished.

The scramble for appointments into lucrative positions has been so fierce among Anglophones that many have been quite ready to sell their patrimony in exchange. I once remarked that some people here can sell their own mothers into slavery for a mess of pottage and was told that I was using unduly harsh language. But all available evidence shows that the metaphor is literally true.

By 1986, it was already clear to all Cameroonians that large scale fraud and looting of the national treasury was threatening our collective survival and that the first condition for a remedy would be to change the autocratic one-party system and democratise. Yet, in March 1990, it was Anglophone ministers and chiefs who, like foolish Moseses, were made to lead their people out, dancing on the streets against democracy and multiparties.

There is a friend of mine here in Yaounde who used to be an uncompromising critic of the Biya regime. Every year he predicted the downfall of the regime before the end of the year in question. He declared that if, *per impossible,* he was to be appointed a minister, he would reject the appointment. Then last year, the impossible happened. He was appointed, not a minister, but something far less. He did not reject the appointment. He said they thought they could buy him over with a post but that he would prove them wrong, from the inside. Today, he is one of the greatest optimistic apologists of the regime even though the collapse he used to predict before looks more imminent than ever before.

Another self-appointed opponent-of-the-regime-friend-of-mine declared that, if one day, he heard his name over the radio appointing him a minister, he would cross the border in less than 24 hours and announce his rejection from the safety of a foreign country. Quite recently, I heard his name, among many others, appointing him, not a minister, but a "chief of service" somewhere. As I used to take him very seriously, I interrupted my lunch and drove to his place, anticipating that he would need my help to drop him at the nearest border. But, to my shock, I met him in an indescribable state of euphoric elation over his appointment. There was already a large crowd of congratulators about him outdoing each other with the firmness of their congratulatory embraces and back-thumpings. Needless to say I sneaked away like a dog out of a funeral hall.

In their recent publication, *PRISON GRADUATE: THE STORY OF CALLING*, Boh Herbert and Ntemfac Ofege graphically provide uswith an insight into the Anglophone problem from one magnified perspective-the CRTV. Any body who carefully reads this book would not need to ask if there is an Anglophone problem and what it is. Boh and Ntemfac have blazed a trail that more Anglophones must be willing to follow if they want to address themselves seriously to the Anglophone problem in this country. He who desires to change an unsatisfactory situation must be ready and willing to undergo some inconvenience or even to take some calculated risks. The hand that opens the door must be willing to go with it as far as necessary. This is exactly what Boh and Ntemfac did in resigning from their glamorous posts at the CRTV. Contrast their forthrightness with the equivocations, subtle rationalisations and fence-settings of some of their other Anglophone colleagues especially those who have obviously drunk deep of the cup of the spoils of office and position and developed the technique of simultaneously running with the game and pursuing with the hunters. In my now nearly five years experience in Cameroon, Ntemfac and Boh are the first Cameroonians I have encountered who have been quite willing to match their words with appropriate action at a critical moment. I doff my hat to them!

In the *Appendix* to their book, which is a collection of the extant "Letters to Joshua" of Cameroon Calling, the authors ask: "But who is Joshua?" and answer: "We wish we knew."

Well, I know who Joshua is and I will share this knowledge with you. Joshua is any young Anglophone who finds the *status quo* unsatisfactory, who rejects it and who is ready and willing to give what it takes, to pay the price, make the sacrifice, to change it. Joshua is every young Anglophone who has vowed not to be like his father, who has cleaned his tongue with a stick, thrown it backwards over the shoulder and sworn that she/he will never stab his people in the back, that he will never eat crumbs from the high table instead of demanding for what is truly his/hers. Joshua is any Anglophone who knows that he/she is a child of the universe with every right to be here.

If not for the Joshuas, we would be celebrating today the sixth anniversary of the burial of the Anglophone educational system and heritage. If not for the Joshuas, Ntemfac Ofege, Boh Herbert, Dr. Hansel Ndumbe Eyoh, Dr. Tatah Mentan, "Mr." Annembom Monju and the rest of their friends would still be languishing as prisoners without any crime, at the Maximum Security Prison, Kondengui, today. It is the Joshuas who on 26th May, 1990, decided to return our country to a multiparty democratic system.

May our Joshuas keep their gaze unswervingly on their ideals and never, like their chicken fathers, be lured into becoming Judases with mere corn. Amen!

Note
1.   Published in *CAMEROON POST* of August 05-12, 1991.

12

The Beginning of the End[1]

'When you see the disastrous abomination, of which the prophet Daniel spoke, standing in the Holy Place (let the reader understand)..." Matthew 24:15

Well, before you mistake me for a preacher, let me own up and introduce myself as a University teacher by deliberate choice and training, although, in my youth, I did, like Paul Biya, more than toy around with the idea of becoming a priest. I should be teaching Philosophy of the Social Sciences right now: 15H 30 Mins, Wednesday, 06-05-92, to a mixed class of about 100 students in Uniyao. But, today, I dare not venture into the University campus. Since last week, the University Students had given notice that they would be celebrating, or rather, commemorating the first anniversary of the occupation of the University campus by the armed forces and the "zero mort" deaths which occurred during that historic event as can, indeed, be testified to by His Royal Highness, the Paramount Chief of Buea.

I have, of course, received the very stylish anonymous tract entitled "OPERATION PAIX SUR LE CAMPUS," addressed to all lecturers, students, and administrative personnel of the University. The tract promises me protection against what it describes as "irresponsible liars and adventurers" called "Students' parliament and their paymasters" who want to disrupt activities in our "noble institution" especially on 06 May 1992, the "historic date when the Auto-Defense liquidated the forces of evil, a diabolic and murderous student parliament." The tract further warns that any absence from campus would be taken as a tacit and flagrant sign of complicity with "illusory- intimidations of rascals and their paymasters." But I am not assured. The terroristic vocabulary conjures visions of fanatical fundamentalism somewhere round the "Fertile Crescent." In fact, I feel more scared of these faceless "protectors" than of the real or imagined dangers from which they purport to be protecting me.

I have learned to be on my guard whenever anyone starts assuring me safety and protection. Since May last year, the University campus has been like a permanent temporary operational military base. A very odd thing which greatly surprises foreign visitors from comparable academic institutions abroad. The University end-of-year for last session were conducted (against all professional advice) in an atmosphere of great tension and turbulence, with soldiers, armed as if for war surrounding all the exam halls. On three occasions I was harassed while going about my legitimate duties by these "protectors" who consistently mistook me for a student. On one occasion, as I was going to supervise the ill-advised exams in one of the halls, they closed in on me, like hunters on a game, with guns and all, under the erroneous conviction that I must be one of the students disrupting the exams. My calm explanation that I was a teacher going to invigilate the exams was not convincing to them and they were about dragging me away when a more convincing-looking colleague, Dr. Chiabi, arrived on the scene and saved me.

In spite of assurances of protection and safety, many lecturers have been attacked in the past 12 months and some have had their cars smashed. The occupational hazards of this once so-called ivory-tower profession are such that any prudent insurance man would surely think twice before insuring the life or property of any University teacher in this country today. You would therefore understand why; when the Association of University Teachers met to discuss the insecurity on the Yaounde University campus, I moved a motion to the effect that the authorities concerned should be told that the "protectors" they had brought to protect us were protecting us by force against our own will and better judgement and that there were rational means and measures not involving soldiers which could be taken to ensure security on the campus. Red caps and guns on the campus, far from being a sign of protection and security are, in fact, the surest sign of abnormality and insecurity.

So this 6th May, no one can convince me to go to the University campus, not even my own Calpurnia. No way! Not again to be caught between the hammer and the anvil. No. Not on the 6th and definitely not in May. I am no clairvoyant, but if the protection, peace and tranquillity that has been promised reigns on campus today, I will put in my resignation, as being too dull and unfit to teach in the University.

We seem to have a destiny with the number 6 and our year ought to begin in May. You need not be superstitious. Look at the evidence yourself. It all began on 6th November, 1982, when, following a mistake induced by the real owners of this farm which we call Cameroon, that is, our Masters, the French, Megida Ahidjo (may Allah have mercy on his soul!) handed dictatorship on a platter of gold to Mr. Paul Biya, an ex-seminarian. On 6th April 1984, Biya had a nightmare, when some people tried to salvage Cameroon from his misrule by the use of the irrational method of brute force. On 2(6) May, 1990, 6 innocent Cameroonians were murdered in Bamenda when Ni John Fru Ndi attempted a more rational way of salvaging Cameroon. And don't forget May *20th* 1972, when Ahidjo believed he had completed the carefully planned conquest and assimilation of West Cameroon.

And here comes May 6th again, and Biya gets another nightmare. You must have read in one form or another Celestin Monga's interview with Robert Messi Messi, former boss of SCB. I have it before me here (in photocopies) as I am writing this. I borrowed it from a friend this morning. There was an amusing incident when I got there to borrow the document. My friend had been reading it and translating for his illiterate mother. He was unable to convey to the old woman in "country-talk" or pidgin the figure 1 billion 250 million CFA which is one of the amounts Messi Messi, on the orders of Madame Biya, is said to have paid to the French-Tunisian architect Cacoub, in July 1988. We struggled together with the idea and I suggested that we should just say that if the money, in ten thousand bills, were carefully packed in the house, it would fill every room up to the ceiling! The old lady shouted in disbelief. But, to be honest how many of us have an idea of what 2.250 billion francs in cash would look like?

I do hope, though, that you did not, like many Cameroonians, pretend to be shocked at Messi's revelations. You aint heard nothing yet, baby! This is evidently only a little tip of the iceberg as, indeed, Messi Messi himself has declared. You wait until we get to SNH. Now, the 2 billion dollar question is: "Why did Caesar ask us for "preuves" when he knew all along that Calpurnia had them in her handbag?" But, of course, what a foolish idiotic question! He *challenged* us to provide the proofs precisely because he was cock-sure they were quite secure in Calpurnia's spacious handbags.

Well, will Caesar cross the Rubicon? I doubt it. I said in the beginning that I was not a preacher. Much less am I a prophet. Look at the *signs of the times* yourself. This looks to me like the beginning of the apocalyptic end which Daniel did not foresee.

Note

1. This and the following 5 papers were published under a column "The Hammer and the Nail" in the short-lived weekly newspaper, *CAMEROON TODAY*, edited by Francis Wache "The Beginning of the End" was published in Vol. 1, No. 001, May 19, 1992.

13

Our Book of Revelations[1]

My priestly hangover is still with me. Well, you don't get over an abortive attempt at "fada-work" so easily, do you? My Bible is never more than a heart-beat away! Last week, I was meditating on Matthew 24:15. Today: my thoughts have taken one giant stride and landed on Revelations, the last Book of the Holy Bible. The Book of Revelations must be one of the least read books of the Bible. You hardly find even scripture scholars who are very eager to discuss it. And perhaps for good reason. Anything revelatory always conjures a feeling of uneasiness. Most revelations are better left unrevealed.

Well, we seem to be landed with a big book of revelations of which the first two chapters have just been read out to us. Shall we hear the rest of the remaining 20 chapters? I hope not! It is unpredictable what that may do to our collective psyche.

I remember Richard Nixon and his "Watergate" mess of the early seventies. At the time, "Watergate" was described as "the greatest scandal of the century." That is because nobody was thinking of Africa or was futurologist enough to catch a clairvoyant glimpse of Cameroon in 1992. Our own "Mvomekagate" would certainly be bidding for the gold medal when all the "gates" of the century eventually assemble for the Olympics.

Aha!, before I continue, I have just remembered that I had a book entitled *I AM NOT A CROOK* which one of my 'friends' borrowed several years ago and has never returned. If you are the one, please, kindly rush the book back to me as I would love to re-read it. Thanks in advance!

Back to Richard Nixon and his Watergate scandal. An apocryphal anecdote has it that, as the Watergate scandal started unfolding, one of Nixon's little kids who, like every other American, had read the screaming newspaper headlines and who, in addition, had been enduring the daily teasing and provocations of schoolmates, came back home from school one day and asked Nixon: "Daddy, are you a crook?" Nixon was touched to a point of tears. So, the next day, he arranged a television appearance in which he addressed the American people in these words: "Fellow Americans, I know all of you are dying to know whether your president is a crook. Well, I assure you that *I am not a crook*. Long live the United States of America!"

He was lying, of course. But he must have calculated that a lie at a time like that was a lesser evil than continuing to keep quiet. Some silences are so loud and so incriminating that any gaff would be preferable. You know, like the guy who was caught last year right here in my "quartier" stealing clothes from the washing line. The fellow said he was only helping to remove the clothes because rain was threatening, even though the sun was actually blazing at the time.

After doing many things wrong, Nixon finally did something right. He resigned. By so doing, he ensured that the "Book of Revelations" of his executive crimes would not be completely read out to the public, which would certainly have happened during the proceedings of the impeachment which was already underway. By resigning, he saved his children, relatives, admirers, friends, and supporters a lot of unnecessary anguish. Just imagine that someone you have idealized and idolized and taken for a saint and superstar, is uncovered as being nothing but a common criminal! The result would surely be irremediable despair.

There is no doubt that our own Nixon was generally perceived in the light of a political superstar, if not a living saint, by most Cameroonians in the years between 1982 and 1985. Things started nose-diving for the worse around 1986 and, if he had been a wise person who could read the signs of the times, he would have resigned then. Had he done so, he would surely have remained a hero in the consciousness of most Cameroonians. But he did not. And when rumours started circulating that the economy, which only a few years earlier had been receiving triple alpha ratings from international economic experts, was in bad shape, he went on national television and pompously declared: *"Le Cameroun se porte bien."* He must, however, have been right at the time, considering that the pillage and rape of the banks and other parastatals took place mainly between 1986-1989. By 1987, he surprised everybody by opening his budget speech with the ominous warning: *"L'année 87 sera difficile.*" Since then, it has been one catastrophic blunder after another up to the present. Why it has never occurred to him that the best option, both for him and the country, is to throw-in the towel, surpasses all understanding.

The first two chapters of the Book of Revelations of the Biya regime have just been read. Chapter one opens with the Messi Messi affair. By the way, some Cameroonians are trying to paint Messi Messi in the colours of a hero. He is evidently no hero but himself a common criminal, fighting like a fly caught inside a bottle. A banker who received an international trophy for his banking acumen cannot give any convincing excuses for transferring 1.250 billion francs of public money to a private account on the telephone orders of a jobless woman.

The second chapter is the presidential plane affair in the U.S.A. Unlike the first chapter, over which the regime has maintained a disquieting silence, official comment has been expressed on chapter two. The Cameroon ambassador to the U.S.A. has issued a release repeatedly read over the official media stating that the plane was not caught with hard drugs but only with counterfeit Dollars which were duly issued by a commercial bank here in Cameroon. That is a very alarming statement, which confirms what those of us with a sceptical bent of mind would have continued treating as a rumour. So our banks are actually issuing out counterfeit currency!? From where does the money get into the banks? Has any bank manager been arrested and detained or tried? Are we supposed to be consoled by the fact that our presidential plane was not carrying cocaine and counterfeits but only counterfeits? If it were an ordinary Camair plane we should not be unduly alarmed. But this is our presidential plane. Again, if the source of the counterfeits were some private small-time criminals we shouldn't be unduly surprised. But we are talking here of our commercial banks. Furthermore, counterfeiting and drug trafficking are as closely connected and organically related as stealing and lying. A certified thief cannot claim not to be a liar nor vice versa. These crimes: lying, stealing, counterfeiting and drug-trafficking are siblings and murder is their first cousin.

Shall the remaining 20 chapters of our Book of Revelations be read? Your guess is as good as mine. During the 20th May tomfooleries, I was just hoping that our *oga* might just seize the opportunity to assure the Nation that he is not a crook, then thank everybody for giving him the opportunity, these past ten years, to serve (himself), but that, since things are getting rather messy, and he can no longer see his way clearly, he was hereby handing back our mandate to us, Long Live Cameroun!

Note
1.   The Hammer and The Nail," *CAMEROON TODAY*, vol. 1. No. 003, June 8, 1992

14

Cameroonians are Unshockable[1]

The late seventies and early eighties were a period of remarkable relative prosperity and optimism in Cameroon. The Cameroon economy looked so buoyant and so promising that it attracted the favourable critical appraisal of the usually highly sceptical Western economic experts. Cameroon was the show-piece of Africa, an oasis of stability, security, peace and tranquillity in a desert of instability, insecurity, turbulence, famine, draught, pestilence and economic chaos. This peculiar situation of Cameroon, of which the peasant farmers were the unrecognized creators, contributed in no small measure to make the one-party dictatorship look plausible. Ahidjo, who in retrospect, can be credited with a certain modicum of economic prudence, political wisdom and personal integrity, rode on the crest of this happy situation as an unchallenged and unquestioned potentate, to the extent that no one raised an eyebrow when he singled-handedly selected his own personal successor-in-dictatorship in the person of the then Mr. (now Dr.) Biya in 1982. Cameroonians were a content people to the extent that most of them spent most of their time drinking, dancing and coupling, if not copulating.

I remember coming home on holidays in 1982 from the University of Ife (now Obafemi Awolowo University, O.A.U), Nigeria, where I was teaching and researching for a Ph.D. of the University of Ibadan. I was so impressed by the contrasts between Cameroon and Nigeria then that I nearly abandoned my Ph.D. research project by not returning again to Nigeria. By that time Nigeria was already fast becoming a hell on earth. Misgovernment and kleptocracy, tribalism and sectionalism etc. had taken their toll on a once very promising country which was now heading straight for the abyss. The insecurity in Nigeria in those days was such that once you crossed the Mfum still alive, you usually sat down to breathe a long sigh of relief and you could literally hear your nerves and muscles relaxing. The contrasts in road infrastructure and transportation facilities were, of course, breath-taking in the reverse direction. But if you did manage to reach within, say, five kilometres of your village, you could confidently leave all your luggage by the road-side and go on by foot to ask relatives to go and help carry the luggage. In the early eighties I used to refer to Nigeria as "the ugly giant of Africa." It looked to me like the country beyond all others where death had a hundred hands and walked by a thousand pathways (road accidents, armed robberies, riots, lynchings, arsons, kill-ajid-goes, ritual murders, etc.)

I remember following some friends to a night club in Bamenda during my 1982 visit. They just parked their car by the road without locking it and we went into the night club. When I remarked that if you did a thing like that in Nigeria the car would surely have disappeared before you came out, my friends shouted incredulously: "Ah-ah Massa, how person fit steal a whole motor! ?" That was Cameroon barely ten years ago.

Today the situation in Cameroon is much worse than anything Nigeria has ever known. Both armed robbery and car thefts, spear-headed by members of the armed forces, have become daily occurrences in Cameroon. Ordinary murders are so rampant that you are taking your life into your hands each time you step out of your house after dark, whether you are going *'cumpe'* (*cum pedibus*) or by taxi. Not long ago, the wife of a SOBAN was brutally murdered in a taxi she boarded around 8.00 p.m., here in Yaounde. Looking at her severely mangled body lying in state, one could hardly believe that this had happened in Cameroon. Today, even Churches are raided by robbers on a nearly daily basis, a thing unheard of in our recent or remote past. Arson has become the order of the day everywhere. Talk less of burglaries, pick-pocketing and ordinary stealing.

What all this clearly shows is that the pilots of our national ship are no longer in control and should, if they were wise, hand over the steering, in their own as much as the interest of the nation as a whole. A government which can no longer guarantee ordinary everyday peace and security for its citizens has no more right to continue clinging onto the reins of power, especially in a situation where several credible "shadow governments" are willing to take up the challenge of leadership. In such a situation, the citizens have the moral duty to "encourage" the aberrant regime in every way possible to vacate the seat of leadership. And if, in addition to what myopia and lack of insight might lead us to mistake for objective happenings resulting from divine anger or something, it also becomes an open secret that neither Caesar's wife nor Caesar himself is completely above suspicion, then they should not even wait for "encouragement" before quitting. If they are wise. But, in our case, the insensitivity of the ruling junta, which borders on contempt for the citizenry, is matched by the apparent unshockability of the citizens themselves.

President Biya once wondered how 12 million Cameroonians could hold a national conference. Following certain recent "revelations" one was almost certain that the practical plausibility or otherwise of that prospect would be demonstrated when 12 million Cameroonians rose up like one man to knock at the gates of one of the palaces of their "fon of fons" with a single roaring question "Mbe Mbe, is it true, is it true??" But Cameroonians seem already quite unshockable. Not even a rumble from 12 million breathing souls, not even from the *ngwerongs*! What a shame, what a shame to be numbered amongst Cameroonians!

Note

1. "The Hammer and the Nail," *CAMEROON TODAY,* Vol. L No. 004, June 22, 1992.

15

From Unshockability to Exaggerated Credulity[1]

L ast time I was talking about the apparent unshockability of Cameroonians. This unshockability is complemented by exaggerated, credulity, the disposition to believe any rumour, no matter how fantastic or far-fetched. These two qualities, credulity and unshockability, manifest themselves not only in the big events but also in the infinitesimal details, all across the board.

A few random instances. On Saturday, May 9th, 1992, a little incident occurred at the University of Yaounde that is very symptomatic of the actual state of things in the country at large. University lecturers, who along with all other Cameroonians have only recently awoken from over 30 years of slumber, have been trying to address themselves to those issues which their calling and training and the taxpayers' sweat make their bounden duty. Well, the University dons have since tried to organize themselves into a professional body worthy of its name. One of their first projects has been to produce a blueprint for salvaging higher studies in Cameroon generally, and the University of Yaounde particularly. Tertiary education in Cameroon is in complete shambles. Everyone knows this. What reigns supreme at this level of our educational system can be aptly described in one single word: FRAUD! What we are shamelessly calling a University here scarcely possesses any of the identification marks of a University, first among which are freedom of thought and expression.

In addressing themselves to the problems of higher education, the University teachers could be said to be fulfilling a very patriotic duty. It is, moreover, their field of expertise and they should surely know what they are talking about. Their blueprint is a document entitled: *THE UNIVERSITY IN CAMEROON: AN INSTITUTION IN DISARRAY.*

Although the errors in the English version of this "White Paper" are no credit to our bilingualism or to proofreading, the substance is such that it is nevertheless quite clear that this is the work of people who know what they are talking about. Their honesty and sincerity of purpose are beyond question. This is the sort of work that an earnest government might have spent millions to hire "experts" to do. One would therefore have thought that a document of this nature would be the first Epistle to any Titus really desirous of salvaging our University system. But a conference on the problematic of Higher Education was actually recently organized without as much as a mention of this document. Do we really expect to be taken seriously?

Now, University teachers have planned to launch their book on the morning of 09/05/92. But there was a snag. The head of their institution, who one would expect is one of them (?) reportedly does not recognize the University dons as a group although, apparently, he does recognize them as individuals. Can a collectivity be different from its components? Can a whole be more than the sum of its parts? In any case, is the nonrecognition of a thing an index of its nonexistence? These are rather metaphysical questions. Whatever be the correct answers to these questions, the Chancellor of the University forbade the University lecturers from launching their book, and ordered the doors of the hall where the launching should have taken place firmly locked. Not to give up at the first hurdle, the dons decided to make the best of a bad situation by having their launching ceremony under a tree. But for every action, as they teach in elementary physics, there is an equal and opposite reaction. The reaction this time, whether equal or not but certainly opposite, was soldiers dispersing the dons at gun point. Luckily no shot was fired. But how can we rationalize this situation? Except, perhaps, to say that ruling by sheer physical force needs no rationalization. The most significant thing, however, is that no one within the University community was unduly shocked by this event. The event was apparently taken as being rather in the nature of things. Which all goes to show how unshockable we have all become.

I've heard some students of Uniyao ask cynically of their Chancellor: "Which school the man attend sef?" Well, no one seems to know. And they would conclude: "You think say if na Sasse or Bali or Sacred Heart he be comout he for de do so?"

This, of course masks the fallacy of association or non-association. Individuals should be judged from their actions and performance, not according to *where they do or do not come from*. Those who for 30 years have cried for an Anglophone Chancellor at Uniyao should not fly to conclusions but should take their time and draw their conclusions on the basis of available evidence. What needs no waiting to be said is that co-operation between the Chancellor and the corps of teaching staff is an absolute desideratum for salvaging the University of Yaounde in particular and Higher education in general.

Regarding credulity, it is really unbelievable what rumours Cameroonians are presently capable of believing as well as peddling. I don't know how long a short visit is supposed to last. But the latest "short private visit" of our head of state abroad seems to have lasted too long. To the extent that the most unbelievable rumours are flying all around the country. Although personally I would rather bet that Dr. Biya is in France, his second home, persistent rumours insist that he is in the USA. Not only that, but that he is there standing trial in connection with drug pushing. Some even claim that, like Norriega, he has been sentenced and imprisoned. Some even claim that a video tape of the trial is already available in Cameroon.

These rumours have an explanation but not a justification. The explanation

is that the life of a public figure is a life in the public glare, willy-nilly. That is one reason that people with skeletons in their cupboards should shun public office. But it is unjustifiable to claim to know what you don't know. On the other hand, it is insufficient to say of a public figure, any public figure, that he has gone on a short private visit abroad without specifying the place and duration of the visit. If he is going for a holiday in Barbados for two weeks, why not say so? The price for being a public figure is living a life in the public glare. May the present and future rumours be put to flight by a simple and accurate statement of the facts. Amen!

Note

1.   The Hammer and the Nail," *CAMEROON TODAY,* Vol. 1, No 0005, July 7, 1992.

16

For the Attention of my Students[1]

I must try my best again to convince you of the following thesis: all formal education involves the acquisition of skills, whether physical or mental, practical or theoretical. A certificate is merely an attestation that such skills have been imparted on the one hand, and acquired, on the other.

The academic session has once more come to an end and many of you are running around helter-skelter, trying to make the best of a bad situation. I warned you at the beginning of the school year! For course-work some of you received 02/20. That is what you deserve because that is what you earned. Just as some of your own classmates received 18/20 because that is what they deserved. I don't *"give"* marks to students. Every student "earns" his or her own marks by his/her work.

Note that when students do very well, they always praise their own intelligence. They proudly say "I made so much in such and such a subject." But when they fail, they invariably blame the teacher: "Don't mind that man, boh; very wicked somebody! Do you know that he gave me only so much!?"

How come you are only now realizing that you were repeating the class and in danger of "burning your mandat?" The boys are again coming with their usual cock and bull stories and the girls with their usual crocodile smiles in an attempt to convince me to change what my own hand had written. I tell you: *Quod scripsi, scripsi!* (What I have written has been written). What principle of action do you expect me to appeal to in changing your marks arbitrarily? You are not the only one who received 02/20. Should I equally change the mark for all who fall in your category? Then what about those who received 03, 04, 05, etc? By Jove, if I follow your suggestion, I would have to give everyone 20/20 and then we would have to close shop. End of formal education for everybody! We would just have to call everyone a "doctor." What would be the use of formal schooling?

In my teaching career I have never taken my own hand to give a student a mark I believed she/he did not deserve. If my mother ever takes my course, she will get the mark she deserves, no more, no less. Nor friendship, nor love, nor blood which they say is thicker than water, nor water which though not as thick as blood, finds its way more easily through impermeable substances, can move me to bear false witness against my neighbour. No one does you a favour by giving you a false testimonial.

Useful skills are never easy to acquire. And when you fall short of acquiring them, there is only one thing to do: try, try, and try again until you succeed. But if you are really beaten in the end, turn to something else. Remember, there are always alternatives even to the alternatives themselves! Believe me, it is better to be a good carpenter or bricklayer than a poor philosopher. As a matter of fact both carpentry and bricklaying are superior to philosophy.

I shouldn't blame you entirely. We live in a society which is seriously sick in *capite et membris* (from head to toe). We live in a country where fraud and corruption have been institutionalized, consecrated and sanctified as national religions. Don't some of my professional colleagues do exactly what I am boldly telling you I cannot do even over my dead body? How often have we not seen pretty damsels who never even followed any lectures pass with flying colours; certified as graduates with beautiful empty heads in exchange for their willingness to "obey the law of gravity" in some "short time hotel" with their teachers!?

Don't get me wrong. I have nothing against beauty or love or even sex. I'm also a true descendant of Adam, and a pair of pretty legs never leave me completely indifferent. I cannot categorically state that, given the chance to be Adam, I would not do what he did to Eve. My problem is that I fail to see the connection between that and bearing false witness.

There's everything to be said for merit and, if we don't try to install a meritocratic system, we are all heading for hell on earth in this country. It is in your interest and in everybody's interest that meritocracy should reign supreme. Help to bring it about that it does reign. Shun injustice and never *beg* anybody. When you're sure that you're right, always *demand*. Remember that education is a life-long process which admits of no short cuts. Bernard Fonlon (1924-

1986) the most remarkable Cameroonian in recent memory, spent over 30 years continuously as a formal student, and the rest of his life as an informal student.

Note
1. "The Hammer and the Nail," *CAMEROON TODAY.* Vol. 1, No.006, July 24, 1992.

17

Revelations Chapter 3[1]

or "INVESTIGATIVE JOURNALISM," the gold medal for
this year will surely go to *LA NOUVELLE EXPRESSION.*"
In this regard, the newspaper is poised to equal any other,
anywhere in the world. As I predicted, the entire 22 chapters of our
"Book of Revelations" will come tumbling, one by one, until the
very last chapter, apparently. Well, no problem. Are we not already
unshockable? Our consciences have become rough, hardened and
impenetrable, like the outer skin of a crocodile.

La Nouvelle Expression has read for us, in a loud and clear voice,
the third chapter of the book of our National Bible of Shame and
Disgrace. Except that we have become quite shameless too. Every
successive chapter of our Book of Revelations will be more revealing,
more unbelievable, than the preceding. Here we are shouting: *crise
économique, crise economique* everywhere. We have been made to tighten
our belts, and taxes are being collected from impoverished citizens
by sheer physical force, at gunpoint. But the high priests of the
battle against the *crise* economique are the ones having shamelessly
large helpings from the diminishing national cake, not before but at
the very height of the crise. So, imagine what must have been done
before the onset of the *crise* to cause the *crise*. This is a situation that
the collective conscience of any epoch in any society should not be
allowed to gloss over. We owe it as a bounden moral duty to
ourselves and to future generations, our own progeny, to address
ourselves to such a lethal virus.

The question that really needs to be asked is this: "Is there any
Cameroonian who, given the chance, would not sell this whole
country to the devil for less than thirty pieces of silver?" Well, that
is only a question. The impression one really gets is that, when all is
told, it may turn out that there is scarcely anybody within the ranks
of our incumbent rulers who could not sell all of us to the devil if
she/he got a good offer. Or else how do we explain the complete
lack of reaction, talk less of indignation, the acquiescence that
borders on complicity, the strenuous efforts to hide the evidence

and the ruthless methods to suppress its leakage anywhere? Just more questions. Maybe you yourself ate *Camtraco* rice today. If you did, you too are far from being a patriot.

I remember with horror the Lake Nyos disaster of 1986. No sooner had it occurred than some newspaper in the U.S.A. came out with the allegation that, far from being a natural disaster, it was a surreptitious test of the neutron bomb, arranged by the American C.I.A. with the complicity of certain Cameroonian authorities. Some Nigerian newspapers picked up the story. But in Cameroon, we laughed at such an incredible story as being too puerile and far-fetched, too fantastic, too science-fictionic to merit even a passing thought. But should any coherent theory of explanation be ruled out for any putative event before the correct explanation has been demonstrated beyond all reasonable doubt? In the case of Nyos, no such correct theory has been forthcoming, as can be seen from the serious disagreements between the various groups of white "experts" who came to investigate the disaster. We will probably never know the actual cause of the Nyos disaster. But now, with the profit of hindsight, and within the context of our unfolding Book of Revelations, the question to ask now is whether it is impossible for people, who have done the sort of things that we have come to know to have connived with diabolic foreigners to organize such a disaster for substantial material rewards? A question too many? A foolish evil thought? You be the judge. I would not assert what I don't know. I only evoke logical possibilities. The United State of America (the world champion of democracy and liberalism) has demonstrated a very suspicious partiality in its attitude towards Cameroon, by comparison with other African countries. In places like Zaire and Kenya, the U.S. has moved very decisively and unequivocally in its support of the process of democratisation and the dismantling of the structures of dictatorship. But when it comes to Cameroon, it has been equivocation all the way. In the U.S.A. the most revered, almost sacred, thing is the Constitution. So why has the U.S. been willing and ready to ignore the fact that the Biya regime has stubbornly refused to start its loudly trumpeted democratisation process with an acceptable Constitution and Electoral Code? For, according to Leonard Robinson, the U.S. Deputy Assistant Secretary for African Affairs, in a News Conference at the American Cultural Centre, Yaounde, June 18, 1992,

"..the United States did not participate in any way in your elections for the National Assembly. We did not send observers. We persistently advised the government - we recommended to the government that the elections be postponed so then the electoral code, voter registration and some of the other issues that were of concern to opposition parties and entities within the country could be resolved."

All these concerns were flagrantly ignored and yet the U.S. inconsistently believes that the National Assembly is democratically representative.

In Cameroon, the U.S. has, uncharacteristically, been quite willing to stand idly by and watch, hands akimbo, excessive repression, abuse of human rights/freedoms and incredible official corruption. The above-mentioned press conference was very telling indeed. Asked about the disparity in the United States' policy in Africa, Mr. Robinson appealed to the concept of diversity *but*, all through the press conference, his attempts to hold brief for the Biya regime were only very thinly veiled. His *"the press has to be beyond reproach... the press must be responsible... If you can't prove it, if you can't document it, don't print it,"* clearly re-echoes Mr. Biya's defiant "Est-ce qu'il y'a des preuves?" But, when the proofs and documentation are proffered as by *La Nouvelle Expression*, the papers are wantonly seized right in the printing houses.

Asked about the case of the Cameroonian presidential plane which was caught in Savannah, Georgia, with counterfeit money, Mr. Robinson first remarks that it sounds like a question from the opposition! before dismissing it as a "non-event" because a very insignificant amount of money was involved. Further asked about the money stolen by African leaders form their impoverished countries and stashed in Europe and America, the Assistant Secretary equivocates *inter alia:*

"it would be very difficult for us to interdict or to block such funds from being transferred to, let's say, Swiss bank accounts, because usually these transactions are done secretly and we have no knowledge of when the transfers actually take place."

So there are secrets which are not within the reach of the famous C.I.A?

The name of the United States foreign policy is "rational self-interest," a policy that other countries would do well to adopt for themselves too. In our case the tragedy is that we don't even have an idea where our interest lies. The Americans are advising us, "in our own interest," to devalue our currency. The French are also advising us, "in our own interest," not to devalue it. Since one and the same action cannot be both in our interest and not in our interest at the same time, it should be clear that our advisers are advising us in their own respective interests under pretence of altruism and philanthropy.

Are the Americans, in their own interest, helping us to sweep our dead rats and cockroaches under the carpet because of petroleum and industrial free trade zone? Yet another question. One gets justifiably worried sometimes. On 10/07/92, the ex-Panamanian president, Norriega, was sentenced to 40 years in prison by a U.S. court for drug trafficking and racketeering. While not denying the charges on which he was convicted, the convict declared that he was a political scapegoat; that the United States had turned against him simply because he had refused to allow U. S. troops in Panama forever. Who would now believe a prisoner? In any case, no such possibility of patriotism here. Our Noreiga would gladly hand over the entire triangle to the Yankees for ever. God save Cameroon!

Note

1. "The Hammer and the Nail," *CAMEROON TODAY*. Vol. 1 No. 007, August 13, 1992.

18

Our Mungo Bridges[1]
(Or What Separates West Cameroonians From East Cameroonians Most Tellingly)

On 11th February 1961, the United Nations conducted a plebiscite in what was then called "British Cameroons," comprising Southern Cameroons and Northern Cameroons. The choice placed before the "British Cameroonians" was straightforward and unequivocal:

(a) Do you wish to achieve independence by joining the independent Federal Republic of Nigeria?

OR

(b) Do you wish to achieve independence by joining the independent Republic of Cameroon?

Southern Cameroonians voted overwhelmingly (70.49%) to achieve independence by reuniting with their "brothers" of "French Cameroons" who had gained independence as "La Republique du Cameroun" the year before (January 1st 1960). Northern Cameroonians, on their part, voted to achieve independence by remaining as a part of the independent Republic of Nigeria which itself had gained independence on October 1st 1960.

In an extremely sagacious aphorism, one of the traditional rulers of the grassfield, Fon Achirimbi the Second of Bafut, is reported to have remarked that the choice placed before "British" Cameroonians by the United Nations was a choice between "Fire and the Deep Sea." The traditional sage was clearly hinting that there was an escape between the horns of the dilemma, a *tertium quid*, between the alternatives presented by the United Nations. But neither the United Nations itself, for some unfathomable reason, nor the political leadership of "British" Cameroons, made up mostly of primary school-teachers-turned-politicians, seemed to see this third option.

Be that as it may; in an address to the nation on May 31st 1961, President Ahmadou Ahidjo lamented what he later described as "the amputation from Cameroon of an important part of its territory and population" and declared June 1st a day of national mourning. He even went as far as the International Court of Justice in an attempt to reclaim Northern Cameroons, but without success. He, however, continued to express the hope and confidence that "our eight hundred thousand brothers outside frontiers" would be with us in spirit until they could completely rejoin us again in body.

One of the greatest ironies of our history is the fact that today Southern Cameroonians have virtually declared 11th February a day of mourning for the disastrous mistake they committed on that day. The "National Day of Mourning for Northern Cameroons" died a natural death because those we were purportedly mourning for were not themselves mourning but were satisfied and happy within the Federal Republic of Nigeria. And yet, it might be a fact that the plebiscite was rigged in Northern Cameroons.

Now, if we try to address ourselves to the question why Northern Cameroonians are quite content within Nigeria whereas Southern Cameroonians would, for the drop of a single pin, quit "La Republique du Cameroun," we may learn a lot of salutary lessons. The crux of the matter is what separates West Cameroonians most tellingly from East Cameroonians.

Let us begin from the frivolous and work our way slowly towards the sublime. For those of us who were still in primary school at the time of Reunification, the first impressionable difference was simply that East Cameroonians were writing the name of our country, CAMEROON, as "*CAMEROUN*." Where we said "Federal Republic of Cameroon," they went about it in a rather roundabout manner, adding unnecessary vowels, and syllables, thus: "*La Republique Fédérale du Cameroun.*"

Their primary school pupils, who went to school in multicoloured dresses of all types, shapes and sizes, looked more like village urchins or urban delinquents than school children.

Their secondary school system was completely incomprehensible to us. While in secondary school we started, logically, from Form One and ended with A/Levels in Form Six, they started their own in Form Six (*Sixieme*) and, after finishing with Form Two (*Second*), they graduated with the "*Baccalaureat*" in what sounded like some deadly illness: *Terminal*!

A West Cameroonian secondary school student visiting an East Cameroonian secondary school could get thoroughly confused. While he may only have smiled to hear his East Cameroonian counterparts calling Breakfast "Small Lunch" (*Petit Dejeuner*), he could not understand why they addressed their teachers as "Mr. Professor"' and even called Reverend Fathers "Mr. Priest"! (*Monsieur l'Abbé*).

In class, East Cameroonian secondary school students are extremely undisciplined, unruly and rude to their teachers, but, individually, outside the classroom, they are extremely polite, submissive, even worshipful.

This attitude is earned over to the University. A casual visit to any of the lecture halls (*amphitheâtres*) of the University of Yaounde would illustrate this. There, as the teacher is busy rambling away and trying to shout above the general din, students are busy doing all sorts of imaginable and unimaginable things: some listening with rapt attention, others sleeping; some drumming on the benches, others whistling; some dancing, others laughing: some shouting like fans at a football match, others eating or smoking; some standing with their backs squarely to the teacher, others engaging in sundry preliminaries of erotic love; right there in the lecture hall! If you have never found yourself in any of the big lecture halls of the University of Yaounde during lecture time, you would surely think that I am exaggerating. A secondary school classmate once came looking for me in my office which is in one of the biggest of these amphitheatres I am talking about. I was not there. He decided to wait. And, to while away the time, he cautiously entered the amphi. He was stunned!

I teach both francophone and Anglophone students and their respective attitudes and comportment are miles apart. An Anglophone University student is generally disciplined and respectful in class but, outside of the classroom, she/he is likely to treat the teacher with an attitude of equality bordering on disrespect. The reverse is the case with his/her francophone counterpart. Refused a favour, an Anglophone student is more likely to go away to complain (and maybe curse the teacher) among his peers. A francophone student is more likely not to accept "no" for an answer, and would continue begging and pleading and repeating his/her request, with tears, if necessary, until the teacher gives in.

I once received the following two letters (requêtes) from two students who had failed submitting their assignment on time, knowing fully well that I am very strict on such matters. The first is by a francophone student and the second by an Anglophone student. Judge for yourself if the different attitudes I've been labouring to describe above are not, at least partially, clearly reflected in these two letters.

The Francophone student wrote:

> J'ai l'honneur de venir très respectueusement auprès de votre haute bienveillance solliciter une indulgence de votre part pour avoir remis mon devoir en retard (cause de maladie) et dans ces conditions peu élégantes.

> Veuillez m 'excuser, Je vous prie, comprenez mon impatience et mon souci. Comme vous n'étiez pas au bureau, J'ai trouvé pour seul moyen d'envoyer mon devoir sous la porte. Je sais bien que cette attitude vis-à-vis de mon professeur est coupable.

> Dans l'espoir que mes excuses seront acceptées, veuillez agréer, Monsieur le Professeur, l 'expression de mon profond respect.

The above letter was neatly written in ink on a clean sheet of paper.

The Anglophone student scribbled his with a pencil on a scrap of paper. He wrote:

> Dear Dr. Tangwa,

> This is the third time I have come to explain why I could not hand in my assignment on time but you are **never** around. I was ill when the assignment was due. I will come again tomorrow around 10.00 a.m.

Please, make sure that you are on seat because I hope
to travel immediately after, back to the village to
continue my treatment.

The "Reunification" of Southern Cameroons with *La République
du Cameroun* in 1961, following the United Nations conducted
plebiscite in Southern Cameroons, was an extremely bold, almost
recklessly foolhardy venture. The overwhelming choice of
Reunification by Southern Cameroonians can only be explained by
invincible, or perhaps vincible, ignorance of the French and the
politico-economic and administrative system that they had installed
in all their colonies.

Before Reunification, scarcely any Southern Cameroonian knew
anything about "French Cameroons" beyond the very friendly
refugees who fled from there and the very agreeable flavour of the
beer and cigarettes that smugglers occasionally brought from across
the borders. There were also travellers' tales, tragically misinterpreted
by Southern Cameroonians, which talked about Frenchmen in East
Cameroon engaging in farming and ordinary commercial activities
such as selling meat and fruits in local markets, in sharp contrast to
snobbish English people in Southern Cameroons or anywhere else,
who could never bring themselves to engage in such menial
activities. These stories were generally misinterpreted as an
indication that the French were less racist, more fraternal and
egalitarian than their other counterparts in colonialism.

These illusive, beliefs would have cleared like cobwebs before
an efficient broom if Southern Cameroonians had known a bit of
the realities lying beyond the appearances of the English and the
French and what it is that really makes each of them tick. The most
remarkable fact about the English vis-à-vis the French is that, in
spite of being blood, relations as well as next-door neighbours,
separated by only a narrow stripe of water - the Channel or *La
Manche* - they have never ever seen eye to eye.

Although the Germans have always humiliated the French in
their historical encounters, especially in war, the French would
sooner "do business" with the Germans than with the English. I
don't know of any full-blooded French person who speaks English
fluently, without an easily recognizable accent. You can quote me.

All pure-blooded French people I have-ever heard trying to speak English always remind me of His Excellency Mbella Mbappe, Cameroon's Honourable Minister of National Education, whose bold attempts at English, though commendable in themselves, are extremely annoying within the context of the "Anglophone problem." Not being very fluent in French myself, I am really in no position to judge English people's speaking of French. But then, I have never ever come across a real Britisher speaking French. Quote me again.

In this regard, Cameroonians are far ahead of their colonial masters. Nearly all educated Anglophones can manage French; many are perfectly bilingual in English and French; and those of them who have been co-opted into the ruling clique frequently; display a better mastery of French than English. I am told that even someone like Hon. John Niba Ngu, the *wowoness* of whose French is known to even those who are dumb in Moliere's language, frequently, while talking in English, forgets the English equivalents of words and expressions that come to him very easily in French. Ditto for Simon Achidi Achu, John Ebong Ngolle, Ephraim Inoni, etc.

An increasing number of educated Francophones can also manage English although, among their really heavy-weight public figures, only Bouba Bello Maigari seems to have really mastered English, thanks largely to his seven years of exile in Kaduna, Nigeria. All the other francophone *yeye* big men, who frequently have to resort to English for ceremonial purposes, bulldoze their way courageously and shamelessly, Mbella Mbappelly.

Wilfred Sheed once declared: "If the French were really intelligent, they'd speak English." The French themselves would seem to confirm this judgment. Recently, a German who is fluent in English but speaks no French was employed at the "Institut Pasteur" in Paris in preference to an equally qualified Frenchman who speaks no English. The Frenchman protested vehemently and publicly. To no avail. Mastery of English is an indispensable requirement, even in France, for working in science and/ or technology related fields.

Most Cameroonians don't realize that the term "Frog" by which Anglophones sometimes refer to Francophones is, in fact, the favourite English appellation of the French, related to the fact that the latter cherish eating frogs. The English have captured their national opinion about the reliability of their French brothers and neighbours in the idiomatic expression "to take French leave." But the French have retaliated by translating the same expression into idiomatic French as: "*filer à l'anglaise.*"

There is a book by too English authors, Denise Thatcher and Malcolm Scoot, entitled *The I Hate the French Official Handbook* (Arrow Books, 1992) which opens with the following declarations:

> "The French have no character-that is their distinguishing characteristic. They are spineless, emotional, weeping women to a man. They cannot speak without appearing to conduct an orchestra. They barge, they dither and they squirm...Seldom do they wash or shave, attempting to mask their odours with garlic and some 360 varieties of smelly cheese"

This book is supposed to be indispensable for anyone intending to travel to France because it would help him/her to change his/her mind and go elsewhere instead. Among the 50 "first class" reasons listed by Thatcher and Scoot for hating the French, are the following:

> "French driving; French banks; Everything stopping for lunch; Hairy armpits (female); Handbags (male); Garlic breath (both sexes); Feigned incomprehension when you talk frog; Pretending they don't speak English; Waving their arms around; Their bread doesn't keep; They are cannibals-they eat frogs"

It is a miracle that Anglophones and Francophones in Cameroon have been able to live together peacefully for over three decades. This miracle can be explained by two factors: the remarkable prosperity of the country- under the dictatorship of the Alhaji and the willingness of Anglophone to quietly "stomach" any rubbish and nonsense from their francophone "senior brothers" in the pious misguided hope that things would accidentally, miraculously or by the grace of God evolve in a positive and more satisfactory direction.

When early in 1991 Pius Njawe and Celestin Monga were arraigned before the courts for the crime of "'insulting the President of the Republic" and given a "suspended conviction," I was stunned. Until I read the following in the handbook of Thatcher and Scott cited above:

> "Under the French law of 1881 it is an offence to insult the President of the Republic...In Britain we consider it a cornerstone of our democracy to be able to insult any one we wish."

Substitute "francophones" and "Anglophones" in the appropriate places and the above passage remains true in our own context.

Recently, Professor Joseph Owona sat down and copied the entire 1958 French Constitution (see CamLife Vol. 2, No. 9, July/August 1993) and presented it to the nation as a draft Constitution designed by a committee of experts. Only Anglophones were shocked.

Generally, the most telling difference, the longest Mungo-Bridge, as it were, between *anglos* and *frogs* has to do with their respective attitudes towards *authority*. For the latter, a person in authority can never be wrong. Recall that francophones were not bothered by the clause in Owona's proposed Constitution which states that the President of the Republic cannot be held responsible for any of his actions. For Anglophones, by contrast, a person in authority, while being respected, is always keenly watched with ultra critical eyes and immediately and loudly denounced for any lapses.

These differing attitudes between Anglophones and francophones are directly reflected in their respective attitudes to fundamental human rights and freedoms. Francophones take arbitrary curtailment of their freedoms, state terrorism and wanton abuse of human rights as rather in the normal order of things. But these things are what have traumatized Anglophones in the past three decades, to the extent that, today, the vast majority of them would rather risk mass suicide than suffer a continuance of this state of affairs.

Note

1.   Written in tribute to Bernard Fonlon, at the anniversary of his death.

Part Two

In the Spirit of GOBATA

1

The Stuff Mandela is Made of*

First of all, I throway salute to all Cameroonians in general and readers of CamPost in particular, especially those who have steadfastly refused to adopt the philosophy of "if you can't beat them, join them." Long time no see!

Without bang or splash, I am back, as I promised. When *ngwerong* alias *kwifon* alias *ngumba* retreats to base, some malefactors may rejoice, forgetting the mood and manner of its probable re-emergence.

The past two years have been spent in retreat and silence. There is a time for talking and a time for keeping quiet. And there are things we cannot talk about. And what we cannot talk about, must be passed over in silence.

There is a time to resume talking. This is such a time. Faithful readers of *NO TRIFLING MATTER* by Rotcod Gobota, in its heyday, and of the short-lived *COCKTAIL* by the son of Gobata would surely have been anticipating the advent or return of the Spirit of Gobata. This column will now be signed simply "Gobata." That way we will spare ourselves the nuisance of those who cannot pronounce "Rotcod" without appearing to have water in the mouth. We will equally be sparing those who have never stopped wondering aloud how a father could transform into his own son. They have surely never heard of or pondered the trinitarian doctrine of Christianity. Now, we will just be "Gobata," without any antecedent or consequent because that is the holy spirit that unites the profane Gobata trinity: father, son and spirit-all distinct in their individuality, and yet perfectly united in their unicity and oneness. The body may be limited or even eliminated, but who can restrain or put shackles on the spirit?

Enough of these parabolic rantings. It is the spirit of Nelson Mandela that I want to talk about on this occasion of the rupturing of a long meditative silence, this pentecost day of the return of the spirit of Gobata.

It is clearly an understatement to say that Nelson Mandela towers, head and shoulders, above all contemporary leaders and heads of state. Few contemporary political personae are fit to stand side by side on the same pedestal with Mandela. You can quote me! That is why, wherever he goes, his presence generates so much excitement among the masses and unease amongst his counterpart heads of state. Recently, a British newspaper, in a moment of rare candour, described Mandela as "the greatest statesman in the world." In Germany and France, Mandela's visit generated the same admirative fever. Who can stand beside him without feeling like a counterfeit in the presence of a newly-minted genuine coin? Is it John Minor of Great Britain who recently preferred the continuance of fratricidal violence in Northern Ireland to taking any risk with his re-election? Northern Ireland had come very close to achieving peace after decades of senseless tension and violence. In fact, it can be said that Northern Ireland caught peace by the tail. But peace surrendered its tail in their hands, like a squirrel, and escaped to safety, plunging them back to square one. All because John Minor saw that the prospect of peace in Northern Ireland did not augur well for his chances of re-election. So he insisted on those impossible pre-conditions that could not but ensure a return to the status quo. Is it Boring Yeltsin who unsuccessfully attempted genocide in Chechenya, successfully managed to get re-elect, and is busy pretending to be in excellent health when all indications show that he is terminally ill? Or is it frère Jacques (bis), dormez-vous (bis) Chirac who recently defied world opinion and protests and stubbornly tested nuclear bombs on other people's backyard? Chirac insisted that the nuclear tests were completely safe but could not answer the question as to why, if that was the case, he did not conduct the tests in France.

On the African continent itself, only Nwalimu Julius Nyerere, former President of Tanzania, can look Nelson Mandela straight in the eye, without squinting or blinking and shake his hand firmly, without trembling or shivering, because they are both made of the same stuff. Nyerere is the only African ex-head of state who, while in power, made a transparently honest effort on behalf of his people, did not amass any personal wealth, did not commit or commission any murders, and quit power voluntarily on his own initiative. By contrast, other African heads of state, past and present, can be categorised into four groups:

(a) whole-sale lootocrats   (b) small-scale kleptocrats,
(c) ruthless dictators and   (d) common scoundrels.

One or two may defy this facile categorisation. But some would answer the roll-call under all four categories.

What makes Mandela tick is something very simple: sincere honesty and charming simplicity. He dresses simply and mixes freely with ordinary mortals because he knows that he is himself an ordinary mortal. After nearly three decades in jail for no crime committed, he is completely devoid of any spirit of vengeance and nurses no grudge against anybody. He owns no landed property in the western world, no coded Swiss bank account. He has not stolen from his people and has not commissioned the murder or incarceration of his opponents or enemies. He appeared in court, like any ordinary- citizen, to pray for the legal dissolution of his irretrievably broken-down marriage. Above all, Nelson Mandela has announced his exit from power, after only a single term in office, for 1999, three good years in advance! Let any pretender to a similar profile step forward. It is quite understandable that other African heads of state feel uncomfortable and rather guilty in Mandela's presence. It was, however, a great blunder for the host of the recent OAU summit in Yaounde to shy away from receiving Mandela when the latter arrived for the meeting. But the attempt to make up for this blunder led to an even greater blunder. Using the diplomatic intercession of Cameroon's neo-colonial proprietors, Mandela was persuaded to route his return flight from France via Yaounde-Nsimalen airport. Then we were all told that Mandela had decided to pay a friendly state visit to Cameroon. A "state visit" lasting barely 45 minutes and confined to the airport where he was exclusively entertained by CPDM Mfoundi section dancers! And then, of course, we heard the expected, *ad nauseam*, from the CRTV journalists and "political analysts" – that Biya and Mandela were intimate friends (witness their warm handshake!), that, for all practical purposes, they are twin-brothers, etc, etc.

Showing Biya and Mandela together has only helped in reminding all Cameroonians of one thing: we need and we deserve a president like Nelson Mandela. We must not fail to get one, come next year.

Written 21/07/96, published Tuesday, July 23, 1996.

Note

*   This and the rest of the following essays are from my on-going weekly column *IN THE SPIRIT OF GOBATA* in *Cameroon Post.*

2

Of Prof Ngwafor's Practical Jealousy and Ambition's Sterner Stuff

Please, forgive today's title. It sounds quite un-Gobatalike, but all the "Sasse" in it is drawn from the *SOBA YAOUNDE CHAPTER NEWS LETTER* of June 1996, although the grammatical, spelling and typographical howlers on every page of that issue are very un-Sasse and should make even 0/Level Sasse students blush with shame. In the said edition of the said Newsletter, the editors single out a SOBAN, prof. Ephraim Ndeh Ngwafor, Rector Yaounde University II, for unqualified praise and accord him an interview in which he enunciates his theory of "practical jealousy," among other things.

Asked about the recipe for his "brilliant appointment" and "remarkable success," the loquacious Prof, responded, *inter alia:*

> A man without ambition is no man! I have my own ambition. But one should not be over-zealous. Rather, any young aspirant should have one or two models to emulate. ...I had the opportunity, while young, to mix with a lot of people most of whom were serious. That gave me the occasion to ask myself if I would not like to be like the Lantums, the Ngus ... and of course the answer was always YES! But yes is not enough an answer. You must make much effort and work hard. ... According to TOLSTOY (Russian Writer)... "The good things you see in others could be a reflection of your own soul. " This is what I would like to call practical jealousy. I was so to speak positively "envious" of the prestigious' positions which I saw in the Nassahs, Ngus and others as I played tennis with them. I told myself that I would like to be like them. Today, thank goodness, I am just behind them.

Such, in a nutshell, is Prof. Ngwafor's philosophy of life and recipe for worldly success, based on practically "jealousing" (still remember the Jealous Constitution?) those you admire and would like to be like. This recipe certainly has much to be said on its behalf provided it is appropriately nuanced and qualified. A man (or woman for that matter) without ambitions scarcely exists anywhere on earth. But while it is recommendable, even inevitable, to have ambitions, not all ambitions are worthy. Some ambitions are *inordinate* and some are even morally wrong. Furthermore, not all efficient means that might be used in achieving an ambition are worthy or morally acceptable. Machiavellian methods can achieve any objective faster than fair and morally acceptable methods, any day anywhere. That does not, however, mean that Machiavellism is recommendable, even on purely prudential grounds. Cheating and other types of fraud can lead more surely to success in any examination than studying hard. Hence, some teachers prefer a short visit, be it to a 'short time Hotel" or at home from their students to long answers in the examination. It is easier and faster to get rich by looting, embezzling or stealing than by working hard in whatever domain. But that does not make these Machiavellian methods recommendable or morally acceptable. Cleverness is not intelligence.

In Cameroon, Machiavellian methods of achieving ambitions and objectives have been greatly reinforced by our collective tendency to be professional congratulators and to celebrate every achievement and every success irrespective of its moral worth and the methods used in its achievement. Earlier this year, a young female friend of mine sent me an excited message that, at long last, she had succeeded in her ambition to be admitted into ENS Yaounde, thanks to a certain CPDM parliamentarian. I sent back the response that while I neither doubted her intellectual capabilities nor her full qualification for admission, I could not congratulate her on her admission because it was not the result of any putative meritocratic process. Any semi-literate CPDM parliamentarian can get any stark illiterate of his choice admitted into ENS, a feat most lecturers at ENS itself are quite unable to perform. Generally at the University of Yaounde, as elsewhere in the Cameroon civil-service, it is by far faster and easier for any lecturer to attain promotion by joining the Presidential Majority and constantly prostrating before the

116

appropriate political power-brokers than by teaching well, researching and publishing, which are the sole criteria of academic success elsewhere, as Prof, Ngwafor rightly pointed out in his interview with the SOBA magazine.

Reverberations of Prof. Ngwafor's appointment as "Le Recteur de Yaounde II" and his bold attempts to dismantle a mafia, clean up and install meritocracy in that institution reached me in my retreat resort and I nearly broke my silence (as I once did to write an open letter to the 400 chiefs of the South West who were ranting against the SCNC) to send him a letter of encouragement, but eventually decided against doing so, as it would not have been in the Spirit of Gobata to act from mere hear-say over a distance.

Now I would like to join SOBANS, Southern Cameroonians and Cameroonians in general to congratulate and encourage Prof. Ngwafor. But, unlike SOBA Yaounde chapter, I am not congratulating him for being appointed "monsieur le Recteur." No one knows what meritocratic criteria or otherwise led to his appointment. In 1992, an eminent scholar, Prof. Marcien Towa, who, with Bernard Fonlon, founded the prestigious defunct journal *ABBIA*, was appointed first Rector of Yaounde II and Ngwafor's predecessor in office. In less than one year, he was unceremoniously removed in the same dramatic manner in which he had been appointed. He had evidently been appointed because of his intricately sophisticated and sophistical arguments against the issue of a Sovereign National Conference and his eleventh hour open declaration for the Presidential Majority in the 1992 elections. No one knows what he did wrong or how he stepped on the wrong toes to earn a sack. But he can fall back only on his real achievements which are his academic publications and international reputation.

I am congratulating Ngwafor for his bold attempts at installing meritocracy and academic transparency and credibility at the University of Yaounde II. This is what one of the Ngus (Jacob Lifanji Ngu), one of Ngwafor's favourite tennis partners whom Ngwafor must have been "positively jealousing," tried to do for the University of Yaounde as a whole. But his office was set on fire and he was lucky to escape unhurt. It is only this bold attempt that will be remembered and credited as an achievement if and when Ngwafor were to be sacked in the manner he was appointed. The appointment itself will not be cited with admiration. It is a struggle to extend Southern Cameroons educational values, as exemplified in Sasse and the other secondary schools, to the institutions of La Republique du Cameroun. Who today remembers or credits the Ngu (victor Anomah) most worthy of "positive jealousy" with the fact of having been a minister? But who can forget, ignore or refuse to credit him for the world-renowned results of his medical researches and his truly remarkable humaneness, humility and moral integrity as a physician? These are the real enduring values and sterner stuff of which ambition should be made.

Written 23/07/96, published Tuesday, July 30, 1996.

3

Struggling Non-violently: The Case of the SCNC

Some people claim that the idea *of non-violent struggle* is self-contradictory an impossible idea. This point of view is not entirely without plausibility, in so far as the very idea of "struggling" connotes or includes a notion of violence. Nevertheless, the idea of non-violent struggle is not only coherent but one that has been successfully put into practice many times in many places. Those familiar with the story and struggles of people like Mahatma Gandhi, Martin Luther King (Jr.) etc, would not doubt this fact.

The struggle of the SCNC is one such non-violent struggle that is bound to succeed, if its tempo and momentum are sustained. A non-violent struggle would not be able to even get off the ground, if the cause sustaining it is unjust or in any other way morally unacceptable or questionable. In such cases, resort to violence is the logical alternative from the onset. The struggle of the SCNC is, at bottom, a struggle for a fairer, juster and more democratic Cameroon.

There are three further indispensable dispositions for successful non-violent struggle: a cast-iron determination, patience and endurance in Jobian proportions, if you can recall the remarkable story of the biblical Job. When all these conditions are present, the success of the struggle is almost an absolute certainly. Remember that Nelson Mandela, besides whom everyone now wants to pose in the hope of stealing a bit of his holy hallow, sustained his determination, patience and endurance for nearly three decades before achieving spectacular victory.

The struggle of Southern Cameroonians which started rather timidly and clandestinely as far back as 1966 when His Excellency, Alhaji Ahmadou Ahidjo, imposed a one-party dictatorship in the Federal Republic of Cameroon, gathered underground momentum in 1972 when a "unitary state" was imposed and further acceleration in 1984 when a bold act of assimilation was attempted by simply reverting the name of the whole country from *The United Republic of Cameroon* to that of its francophone component. *La République du Cameroun,* signifying that the to-be-assimilated had now been completely assimilated. But the conceptors, architects and executors of this master-plan of assimilation were forgetting that a subsisting people and their history cannot simply be wiped away with a single stroke of a presidential signature under a decree.

And so in 1993, the struggle boldly came out of its masquerade and shelter, alias the Social Democratic Front (SDF), into broad, daylight with the AAC1, epitomised by *The Buea Declaration* which defined its non-violent character clearly. The AAC2, culminating in *The Bamenda Proclamation* (1994), further sharpened the focus of the struggle and led directly to the depositing of a formal petition against

annexation and for the autonomy of Southern Cameroons before the United Nations Organisation (UNO) in 1995. This petition has so far been neatly locked up in the voluminous drawers of the Secretary General because of Boutros, Boutros Boutros' personal friendship with some powerful personalities who want the case swept under the carpet and because of certain secret deals between frère Jacques Chirac of France and Major Minor of Great Britain. But tune is on our side.

The case against the annexation and for the autonomy of Southern Cameroons is a simple, straightforward and powerfully persuasive one. These trying to confuse the case so as to cover up their illegal and unacceptable acts continue chanting that Cameroon is *one and indivisible.* How did two entities, each of which *ante* 1972 was one and indivisible in its own right become, in collective conjunction, simply one and indivisible in the singular? Meaningless expressions like "one and indivisible" have only *emotive* but no *real* content. No amount of oneness and indivisibility can erase the linguistic, educational, legal and administrative differences between Southern Cameroons and La République du Cameroun. This does not, of course, mean that they cannot subsist harmoniously together as co-operating autonomous entities. In fact, they did between 1961 – 1972. The *Buea Peace Initiative* has spelled out in discussable and modifiable details how this can again be done in very practical terms.

To carry the struggle of Southern Cameroons to a successful conclusion, it is necessary to maintain conceptual clarity all the time and not be distracted or confused by purely tangential matters. It is equally important to keep at bay frustration and unfounded discouraging speculation initiated by enemies of the cause such as "Simon Munzu, Carlson Anyangwe and Ekontang Elad have been bought over and have abandoned the cause." Early in 1995, some Minister in the current regime went abroad to tell Cameroonians everywhere that the SDF was now completely "finished" because Siga Asanga, Ben Muna and Charly Gabriel Mbock had all abandoned Fru Ndi and were preparing to join the CPDM. From what I personally know of Munzu, Anyangwe and Elad, and on the basis of their proven integrity and commitment to the Southern Cameroons cause, I don't believe that anybody or any conceivable amount of money is capable of "buying them over." Each of them is what Bernard Fonlon used to call a *vir probandus* (a tested and proven man) and not a *vir probatus* (a man on probation, still to be tested and proven). Personally, I can recognise most Southern Cameroonians who wouldn't hesitate to betray their own cause if they were offered sufficient inducement from a distance. The Munzu - Elad - Anyangwe trio cannot be counted amongst these unprincipled Southern Cameroonians who can sell their own mothers and children into slavery.

The absence of Anyangwe, Munzu and Elad from the leadership of the SCNC must be circumstantial, although there is no ruling out of the possibility that some of those circumstances might have been induced, forced or cleverly arranged by enemies of the Southern Cameroons cause. I am confident that, wherever they may be, they would each singly and collectively continue the good work that they began and that they performed so well. We owe them an unpayable debt of gratitude for their courage, determination and commitment.

But the struggle must continue, whoever comes or goes. Each and every Southern Cameroonian must be willing and ready to assume leadership of the struggle or, in any case, to continue the struggle until final victory, no matter what may happen or fail to happen in the interim. For this reason, it is foolish to refuse registering on the electoral list on the ground that the coming elections are the elections of La République or that victory will, as usual be confiscated by the dictatorial regime. If a more democratic government were to come to power under the present set-up, it would certainly be more open to dialogue and that would surely make the struggle easier, since at no time do we envisage substituting *the argument of force for the force of our argument.* That victory was confiscated yesterday doesn't mean that it will be confiscated tomorrow, if the right lessons are learned and determined efforts redoubled. In spite of the tricks and intrigues of the ruling regime, some progress was certainly made during the recent Municipal Elections, even though, in some places, some people won by the ballot box and others claimed the victory via tear - gas. There doesn't seem to be any peaceful formula by which the Southern Cameroons cause can be resolved under the present dictatorship masquerading as an advanced democracy. It is in the interest of every Southern Cameroonian to work towards a democratic breakthrough in the months ahead. No one should take things lightly. All hands must go on deck. It is our very survival that is at stake.

Written 31/07/96, published Tuesday, August 13, 1996.

4

Western Democracies and African Dictatorships

Although democracy as a system of governance has acquired the status of a sacred dogma in western political thought and ideology, the western democracies are not as democratic as theory and appearances may lead one to believe. In fact, if we define democracy (as I strongly recommend we should) as any political system in which there is control of power and authority by those who are subject to it, in which the will of the majority prevails but the rights and interests of the minorities are protected, in which the supreme authority is subject to checks and balances and peacefully removable by majoritarian will, then some western democracies are only apparently democratic. If you consider the effects of paid propaganda and the manipulation of public opinion through the electronic media as well as what most western political authorities usually do in a bid to get re-elected, you will not disagree with this statement. From this perspective, many of the Traditional African kingships (fonships), circumscribed as they were by sundry taboos, ritual restrictions and sanctions, were arguably more democratic than some contemporary western democracies. I could write a whole book defending this thesis but that is not necessary for our purposes here and now.

Another point to note is that most western democracies not only support but actually initiated and introduced dictatorships abroad, especially in Africa. Democracy (at home) for westerners has been quite compatible with dictatorship (abroad). From the era of colonisation and empire - building to the present, western countries have reaped the benefits of dictatorship abroad and used them, quite paradoxically, to build and strengthen their own democratic structures. Even western government prefers to have to deal with a single African dictator, for any given country, who can take snap decisions concerning exploitation of any putative resources, than to deal with the majoritarian masses with their inevitably conflicting ideas and interests. It is faster and safer and more profitable, in short, better for business to have to deal with only a single individual. This is why whenever a really popular leader among the *massa damnata,* who actually listens to his people, has emerged anywhere in Africa, he has been frustrated or killed by or with the active connivance of western agents. All the long-reigning dictators of Africa are mere commission agents and pimps of some western powers. Never mind all the noisy theoreticals and theatricals in the name of democracy.

I know what I am talking about and you can quote me as usual. Constituted authorities and people in power everywhere seem, almost instinctively, to act as accomplices of one another against ordinary people everywhere. The way of one big man with another must be one of the inexplicable mysteries of the world. I dare say that this is one plausible reason why many people here were somewhat disappointed with the last papal visitation. Many had been hoping that the successor of St. Peter and inheritor of the fisherman's shoes would, like the no - nonsense OT prophet, Amos of Tekoa, unleash his holy tongue and take the rulers of the land to severe task over the regular and systematic atrocities committed against people of God in this erstwhile oasis of peace called Cameroon. But the Head of the Vatican State simply made some fairly veiled and weak statements and then went to bless, play and dine and wine with our own PW (Prince of Wales).

If we are to believe press reports, is it not his Excellency, Paul Biya, of Cameroon who saved the life of his equal Excellency, Sanni Abacha, of Nigeria during the recent OAU summit meeting in Yaounde by alerting the latter to an assassination plot by some Nigerians? This was a very commendable act by the chairman of the OAU; for the life of a dictator is no less (nor more) sacred and valuable than that of the innocent victims of his dictatorship. But why can the duo not also come together to stop the assassination of innocent ordinary people in this senseless Bakassi conflict? Is the answer not blowing in the wind? It is about time that ordinary people all over the world got up and co-operated and joined hands to protect their collective interests.

The brazenly callous judicial murder, by the Abacha dictatorship, with the tacit connivance of the Anglo-Dutch conglomerate SHELL, late last year of Ken Saro Wiwa: writer / poet / novelist / dramatist

/ human cum minority rights campaigner /eco-environmentalist/ pacifist and eight other Ogonis revealed a great deal concerning what I am talking about here. By the way, let me call the other eight Ogonis properly by their names. Everyone keeps talking of "Ken Saro Wiwa and eight other Ogonis" as if these other eight were nameless entities. This often gives the impression that it is because Ken was a famous writer, etc, that people are so shocked. It is not because a person is this or that that his/her murder should shock us. The other eight Ogoni people murdered with Ken Saro Wiwa on 10th November 1995 are by name: Saturday Dobee, Barinem Kiob, Paul Levura, Nordue Eawo, Felix Nuat, Daniel Gbokoo, John Kpuinen and Baribor Bera. To this list should be added the name of Clement Tusima who had earlier in August 1995 died in detention, bringing the number of these Ogoni martyrs to ten.

I happened to have been in the U.K. when these murders were carried out and I actively participated in the demonstration at the Nigerian High Commission and SHELL headquarters on Saturday 18th November 1995. By the way, no one brought water-cannon or tear-gas, talk less of bullets, to disperse the demonstrators in the name of "*l'ordre publique*" there as would surely have been the case here. There were police people there alright but their main preoccupation was to ensure that no evil-minded person used the demo as a cover for acts of brigandage or vandalism. (TO BE CONTINUED)

Written 03/08/96, published Tuesday, August 20,1996.

Western Democracies and African Dictatorships (Continued)

The real tragedy in the execution of Ken Saro Wiwa and his compatriots is not the mere fact that it was done in contemptuous defiance of the Commonwealth and persistent pleas from all over the world but that the executed people were evidently quite innocent of the purported crime for which they were hanged. As I have once said before, even worse than any imaginable crime is the crime of knowingly hanging a crime on an innocent person. That is why it is well said that it is better for a hundred criminals to go free than for a single innocent person to be punished unjustly. Anyone who had carefully followed the struggle of the Ogoni people against the reckless destruction of their habitat by the Shell oil company in alliance with successive Nigerian regimes knows this very well. Ken and his compatriots were framed for a crime committed, in all probability, by the very people who hung it on them and hanged them for it, with the ultimate aim of crushing the Ogoni nuisance and threat to continued oil exploitation in the area. This is a familiar strategy resorted to by other dictatorships in Africa and their foreign proprietors.

The executions in Nigeria shocked the conscience of a world that is becoming increasingly unshockable. Among ordinary people everywhere, there seemed to be a genuine feeling of outrage. But the reaction of those in power (both political and economic) who were really in a position to do something about the situation left much to be desired. As Americans would say, the bottom line here is that the murder of innocent human beings is still being done and condoned for the economic convenience of some people. If you listened carefully and read between the lines of the rhetoric of western reactions to the Ogoni executions, you would not have failed to realise that many were the crocodile tears of the accomplices of the Abacha dictatorship. Evidently, the western world has made little moral progress in the last five decades. Quote me! "Western power-brokers were talking about imposing sanctions on "Nigeria" and then arguing hypocritically that such sanctions would only harm ordinary Nigerians. This highly hypocritical line of argument was made fashionable under the Thatcher regime of Great Britain in relation to Apartheid South Africa. Putative sanctions should not have been thought of as being imposable on Nigeria but rather on the Abacha junta in Nigeria. As a matter of fact, over 90% of all Nigerians at the time would willingly and happily have gone on a month-long hunger strike if only there was any hope that that would rid them of the Abacha nightmare and give them another chance to attempt genuine democracy.

If a total economic blockade had been imposed by the western democracies on the Abacha regime in November 1995, it would surely have collapsed like a sand castle built by a dull child within a maximum of two weeks. This would have been in

the long-term interest not only of Nigeria but of the rest of the world. But this was not contemplated because of the selfish exploitative economic interests of the USA, Great Britain, France, Germany, etc. The USA stated clearly, shamelessly and without any equivocation that boycotting Nigerian petroleum would harm the economic interests of the USA. Although the executions in Nigeria were clearly calculated and timed to spite the Commonwealth, the reactions at the Commonwealth summit which was sitting at the time were determined by the same Machiavellian self-interest and inevitable quiet complicity of leaders who know very well that they themselves are not different from Abacha. (There are few people of the stuff and calibre of Nyerere or Mandela in power anywhere in the world). That is why they "suspended" instead of "expelling" the Abacha regime from the Commonwealth and pretended that they were giving Abacha two years within which to vacate his dictatorial throne and install democracy. By what magic were they hoping to prevail on Abacha to follow such a time-table? If they could not prevail on him to refrain from committing plain murder, how did they hope to prevail on him to hand over power within two years when, in fact, he is in power precisely because of his previous refusal to hand-over to a democratically elected government?

In stark terms, we can blame Nigeria's predicaments, the predicaments of nearly all African countries, on the following causal factors: the persistence in power of dictatorial regimes which are no more than powerful associations of domestic bandits in connivance and co-operation with western powers which want to continue exploitation of Africa without appearing to do so.

When it comes to Africa, the leaders of the western democracies seem to prefer dealing but with the dictators because of the ease with which economic decisions can be taken. In this case, there is only one single individual, responsible to no one else but himself, to deal with. In this way western democracies combine very well with and are complimented by African dictatorships.

Following the Ogoni executions, I was struck by the care with which all western governmental people chose their words and comments. Their main pre-occupation was, evidently, making the correct statements rather than doing anything. This, of course, corroborates well with the general western tendency whereby more interest and emphasis are placed on accurate reporting of, say, disasters and catastrophes than helping its victims or doing something about them. It is hardly surprising that, within the Commonwealth, the 1991 Harare Declaration has remained a dead letter in spite of the care, precision and clarity with which it was formulated.

The situation in Nigeria is replicated to varying degrees in other African countries. If the Harare Declaration were not a dead letter, do you think Cameroon would have been so easily admitted into the Commonwealth as it was in Auckland in 1995? Had Cameroonians of good will and faith not been hoping that the Harare conditions would help the Biya regime to tidy up its human rights record and raise its liberalisation and democratisation from the level of empty rhetoric and bold pretences where it has remained since 1990? Africans must struggle for the liberalisation, democratisation, and modernisation of their societies without expecting any help or assistance from where they are unlikely to be got.

Written 03/08/96, published August 27, 1996.

6

Tenth Anniversary of a Horrible Year

I am scripting this piece on August 27, 1996, exactly ten years, to the day, since the untimely death of Bernard Nsokika Fonlon whose birthday on November 1 9th I always join other Fonlonians to celebrate under the conviction that, even though the man died prematurely, it was a very good thing that he was born. Fonlon died in Canada on the occasion of his reception of the distinguished honour of a doctorate degree (*honoris causa*) award from a prestigious Canadian University. Fonlon's tragic death coincided with and was preceded the previous week by an unprecedented disaster in which nearly 2000 Cameroonians, over 4000 livestock and countless other animals perished in the Lake Nyos catastrophe of August 21, 1986. Nineteen eighty - six was truly a terrible year for Cameroon and as we remember (as against *celebrate*) the aluminium or tin anniversary of that horrible year, we cannot help shuddering as time cycles often and the number 6 are to be dreaded.

As a sort of advance silver lining or sugar coating to a sad subject permit me to digress a little here and thank my good friend and accomplished Fonlon scholar, Mr. Kevin Mbayu, for drawing my attention to an uncharacteristic but inexcusable error, a veritable slip of the mind in *IN THE SPIRIT OF GOBATA* of Tuesday, August 13. 1996, entitled "Struggling Non- Violently: The Case of the SCNC." In that piece, which I had written under unusual and difficult circumstances, away from my personal library, books and source materials, I did not exactly quote Fonlon upside-down, but, nevertheless, made a culpable reverse substitution of the meanings of his famous expressions: *vir probandus* and *vir probatus* because of my now rather rusty grasp of Latin, owing to time and disuse. It is an error that Fonlon could never have made and that careful Fonlon scholars like Kevin Mbayu would detect at a glance, any day, anywhere.

This column has no direct didactic pretensions, but it would be inexcusable to condone the danger of popularising a factually wrong cliché. Parenthetically, I should remark that I am impressed by the number of writers who love using the very catchy Latin expression of the idea of "a healthy mind in a healthy body" (*mens sana in corpore sano*) but who write it as *mens sano in copore sano* because that is how some careless professors have it in print in their works. So, please, take note and put your records right. A well-tested and proven person is a *vir probatus* while s/he who is still to be so tested and proven is a *vir probandus*. Thanks Kevin!

Incidentally and parenthetically again, the defensible reason for which I sent an excusably slightly insufficiently researched piece for publication was that I did not want the column to miss appearing barely three weeks after its debut. But, quite ironically, the column failed to appear that very week in spite of my costly efforts, because my piece, apparently, did not reach the editors of *CamPost* on time through no fault of mine. At Nkwen in Bamenda on Sunday 11 / 08 / 96 and at Kumbo in Nso on Monday 12 / 08 / 96, some readers of *Cameroon Post* and fans of Gobata nearly lynched me over the absence of *IN THE SPIRIT OF GOBATA* from the latest issue of the paper. Not having seen the said issue myself, I was completely baffled as to what they were ranting about. Are these the inevitable hazards and fair wages of a good columnist? If so, where are its plums and silver linings? But let me take this opportunity and repeat here a "warning" I once issued with regard to the rather short-lived COCKTAIL ... from the son of GOBATA, namely, that this column is subject to interruption, discontinuance or even disappearance without any prior notice, especially if co-operation and encouragement from the *CamPost* management is found at any time to be wanting. I will, of course, do my utmost best as usual and I pledge my word to that effect. But I cannot do more than my best and I will not, at any time, try to catch the wind or square the circle.

Back to our *anno horribilis*, 1986. In spite of Radio and Television noise about this 10th anniversary of the Lake Nyos disaster, a remarkable fact is government lack of interest in the whole affair. The 1986 disaster struck while I was at the University of Ife (now Obafemi Awolowo University) Nigeria, preparing to return to Cameroon within a couple of months, I immediately sent a piece (not unlike the ones you have usually read in my columns) to *Cameroon Tribune* which was published on Tuesday, October 28, 1986. In that write-up entitled "The Medium and Long Term Lessons of the Lake Nyos Natural Disaster" I made two important recommendations, *inter alia*. The first was the necessity to disenclave the region by the construction of an all-seasons motorable road, considering the difficulties that were encountered in trying to get emergency help to the area. The second was the equal necessity for a carefully worked-out resettlement scheme for all those living within a ten kilometre radius of any of our volcanic lakes, considering that neither the exact cause nor probable course and time-table of these explosions is as yet known to us.

But none of these suggestions, which remain valid today, was even considered. Instead, help for the survivors of the disaster sent in by genuine philanthropists was characteristically callously misappropriated. Had the government at the time, undertaken to construct even only ten kilometres of road yearly in the region, a hundred kilometres of all seasons motorable roads would already have been constructed by now. But absolutely nothing has been done, while the President and all the President's men continue hanging on precariously from the rafters of dictatorial power. And recently, to blow smoke in the eyes of the restless populations of this region, they have started repairing the Ring Road as a laterite road so that real roads can be constructed in another region without a loud outcry. Who is fooled?

It is equally significant that, ten whole years after, the real cause of the Nyos disaster has not been determined. It is equally note-worthy that the foreign so-called scientific experts who rushed in here in the wake of the explosion have continued to disagree "scientifically" along curiously national lines. Should we not take a healthy pinch of snuff?

As for dread of cycles of ten, the number 6 and its multiples and divisibles you may or may not have heard, but the President of La République is ill. Would you translate the last phrase of my last sentence into French as: *Le Président de la République est malade?* That is up to you, but your translation could reveal something as to whether you are a true Southern Cameroonian or not. Anyway, if you are still blind, deaf and dumb in Moliere's language, you may not be aware that some newspapers of La République have lately engaged in wild speculations and insinuations about the presidential illness. Some have recalled what happened to Ahidjo in 1982 shortly after a change of regime in France and are pointing an accusing finger in that direction. Others are claiming that he is dying of sheer idleness and that it is very dangerous for an old man to saddle himself with the enviable herculean duty of conjugally satisfying his putative grand -daughter's age-mate. But all these speculative conjectures (which could earn them a prison sentence in any of their *yeye* courts) do not interest me. I say my own that we should really congratulate the authorities for honestly announcing the presidential indisposition, instead of telling us as usual, that he has gone for a short private visit abroad.

Why are they always hiding the illness of people in power? Think of Boris Yeltsin and remember Francois Mitterrand. Is illness a weakness? Is illness someone's fault? Is it a culpable crime to be ill." His Excellency is said to be suffering from severe brain fatigue. Is that not an ailment that could afflict anybody at any time who does brain work such as having to remember the names of all the Presidents of Africa so that when you are shaking their respective hands you would also call their respective names correctly? Imagine the sacrilege of, say, shaking Abacha's hand while saying "Welcome Mandela"! Brain fag is no big deal. In my days in Sasse, many students used to have it from mere swotting and nocturnal "monastics." Have you ever heard of any one dying from mental illness?

Written 27/08/96, published Tuesday, October 15, 1996

7

Where we Should Be Heading

As a freshman undergraduate at the University of Nigeria, Nsukka, which, as they used to boast in those days, is "the very first autonomous indigenous University in all of Africa south of the Sahara and north of the Limpopo," I remember most vividly "orientation week" and all its activities and lectures. Among the lectures, that of a certain Professor which lasted less than three minutes stands out prominently in my memory He simply told us :

> "Welcome to the University of Nigeria / And congrats on your admission. You have come out of the bush and you want to go through this University. You have succeeded in coming out of the bush by yourself. Here we will try to take the bush out of you. It will not be enough to simply go through this University. You must also allow the University to go through you. Welcome to the University of Nigeria!"

This very short lecture, which hides a lot of important and salutary counsels under a witty joke, keeps coming to my mind when I think of the common predicament of all of us, Cameroonians. In the past six years we have gone through a lot of the harsh lessons of experience because of our collective inability to use sheer reason to anticipate our problems and to know the required solutions. Experience may be the best teacher. But in going through these harsh lessons of experience, have we failed to allow the lessons to also go through us? In other words, have we learnt anything at all from the sad experiences of the past six years? Since 1990, when the incumbent regime should, in its own interest, in the patriotic interest of the nation and of all of us, have given up power, having clearly demonstrated both its inability and unwillingness to lead us to an earthly *Nirvana* after nearly a decade since its unblessed advent, the quality of life has been deteriorating alarmingly in all aspects and respects progressively every year.

Cast your mind back to the year 1982, with its euphoria, invincible optimism and promises, and pick any aspect or detail of (individual or collective) life and then compare it with itself in 1996. We have progressively descended from the prospect or, at least, illusion of paradise to the very bottom of the pit, to an earthly hell. Have we gone through all the harsh lessons of life without learning anything from them? If in going through our hard experiences we had also allowed the experiences to go through us, if we had learnt anything at all from our harsh past, we should, by now, certainly know where we are heading.

But the truth is that we have continued drifting like a rudderless ship, and believing in the same illusive promises and palliative solutions that failed us yesterday; rushing out again today, like chickens, for the same corn that caused the wringing of our neck yesterday. Suffering (and smiling?) along with everybody else are those who yesterday received incentives and marched against democracy, maimed and killed to safeguard the *status quo,* or lent their intellect to its sophistical rationalisations and rhetorical white-washings and shit-shinings. I'm filled with pity and sadness when I see the same people who yesterday happily received two thousand francs and marched to congratulate and support His Excellency for reducing salaries, today roaming the streets and enquiring whether a member of the regime is not organising something so that they could join in the hope of getting "'something." I'm filled with pity and sadness that in 1996 there are still Cameroonians who can exchange their ballot paper for a bottle of beer or even half a small bowl of local *kwacha* as is said to have been the case in some parts of the Extreme North during the last Municipal elections. I'm filled with pity and sadness for all of us, for our hopeless teeming youths and for our children with a most uncertain future.

If we had learnt from our experience we should today be firmly headed for a truly liberal and democratic breakthrough, in spite of the reverses and backslidings of the past. Such a liberal and democratic society would be in everybody's better interest, including those who today are clinging on to dictatorship animated by democratic vocabulary and rhetoric. Remember that it was the same very repressive state structures set up by Ahmadou Ahidjo that ensured that he would die and be buried in exile in a foreign country, like a common wretch and nonentity. He didn't deserve such a fate, in spite of his dictatorship. Those who are banking on their marble castles and secret-coded bank accounts abroad should reflect on why ex-Emperor Jean Bedel Bokassa of the Central African Republic (formerly Empire) eventually preferred to face a prison sentence at home in spite of his marble castles and bank accounts abroad. Our country should be big enough to contain all of us, heroes and non-heroes alike. Let our criminals languish in our own jails. Let us opt for a society where no one needs to flee into exile. Let us bury our heroes here and honour them as well as our non-heroes and scoundrels and *spit on their graves*.

It is amazing that a few months from the very important and decisive elections of next year, the long-awaited and highly indispensable *Independent Electoral Commission* (IEC) has not yet been put into place and all of us are sitting down quietly and complacently. In spite of the OAU chairman-ship, it is evident that his Excellency would not opt for transparency in the conduct of elections without considerable encouragement. It is equally amazing that most Cameroonians are still joking with their *right to vote*, the most basic, fundamental and inalienable right in a civil society. For quite flimsy reasons, many people are not registered on the electoral registers. Let them not complain if things don't evolve according to their wishes.

The only right that we have as ordinary citizens is the right to vote out a bad government. We will never be able to know in advance whether the new government we have voted in to replace the bad one would perform to our total satisfaction. But this should be no cause for worry as long as we retain the right to vote it out in the next election should it disappoint our justified expectations. What we cannot afford to do is to help maintain in power a government which has demonstrated its fatal vices and limitations, a government which has failed woefully, again and again, before our very-eyes. The passport to head for where we should be heading in our collective interest, is your vote and my vote, our common action together as common but free citizens who are not in power but who freely elect and mandate those who are to wield power over us. So, please, don't joke with your right to vote. We have collectively passed through the harsh experiences of the past several years together. Let us together allow these experiences to pass through us.

Written 07/09/96, published Tuesday, October 15, 1996

8

In the Spirit of a Zealous Disciple

There is a remarkable story told by all the four biblical evangelists - Matthew, Mark, Luke, and John - about the Passion and eventual crucifixion and death of Christ. It is, in fact, the opening story of the Passion, just after Judas had betrayed Jesus with a kiss. The story is about one of the servants (slaves) of the High Priest who was among the rowdy crowd that had come with clubs and swords to arrest Jesus as if he were some common criminal. The High Priest's servant's name was Malchus. Before anyone could shout "Malchus!," one of the zealous disciples of Jesus had drawn his sword and slashed off Malchus' right ear. But Jesus, who was the one being molested and arrested, cautioned his over-zealous man to put his sword back into its sheath; then he picked up Malchus' severed ear and replaced it back in its place.

Although it is often said that no disciple can be greater than his master, I am always more terrified of the disciples than of the master himself. The master is usually always more reasonable, compassionate and understanding than his fanatical disciples. Beware of zealous disciples because they are always capable, willing and ready to do what the master himself might not even have contemplated. To joke with disciples is to run the risk of having your ears slashed off even before you could finish shouting "disciple" and the master may not be Jesus enough to come to your rescue.

If you happen to be a master, especially one who has prerogatives of providing employment, hiring and firing, running a budget and awarding contracts, then you need never bother about your critics and opponents, talk less of enemies. You can sleep soundly because your numerous disciples (or is it apostles?), both actual and potential, both known and unknown to you, would "take good care" of your possible adversaries, both real and imagined, and only come to report the good work they have done on your behalf.

I remember one occasion, shortly after the publication of *The Past Tense of Shit* (not the book but the article). Some disciples of an unknown though knowable master came making enquiries about

Gobata at my favourite "watering hole" in Djoungolo. Then one day they came back and asked the cigarette seller by the road side where Gobata usually crossed the main road after his drinking spree at his favourite place, parked a heavy truck a short distance away, and waited for the moment the son of man would be staggering drunkenly across the road. Had the cigarette vendor not been a friend indeed and sent a small pickin to whisper that those gentlemen of the other day were patiently waiting in a truck, the intended would most probably have happened. And then the master would have been presented a surprise gift: "Master, that mosquito will never worry your precious sacred ears again. We have taken care of that little noisy troublesome mosquito with a sledge hammer, Master. We love you so much, Master. Allah quo! We love you more than ourselves. Honest to God, Master!" But, as God would have it, the son-of-Gobata, as he was then popularly called, vamoosed without trace through another foot path.

What I have said so far does not necessarily have any direct connection with the rest of what I am going to say. Some time ago (See *In The Spirit of Gobata* of Tuesday, July 30. 1996) I wrote a piece entitled "Of Professor Ngwafor's Practical Jealousy and Ambition's Sterner Stuff," intended to congratulate and give qualified praise to the high public functionary mentioned in the title. But, while Prof. Ngwafor himself has not openly and/or publicly reacted to my qualified praise which came mixed, as usual, with several other both related and unrelated issues (nor was he expected to), one of his admirers (positive jealouser?) has written a rejoinder to my piece. (See *CamPost* of Tuesday Sept. 10 -16, 1996).

If Prof. Ngwafor were to write a rejoinder to my qualified praise of him or to my entire piece, I would respectfully answer him in detail. Most of what I am saying here has got nothing to do *directly* with Pius Kwendi (whom I am not privileged to know personally) whose rejoinder provides the *occasion* but not the entire *focus* of this piece.

My piece on Prof. Ngwafor has brought me more trouble from third parties than I bargained for. I am reliably informed, for instance, that the Executive (or some members thereof) of SOBA (Yaounde Chapter) are quite upset with a passing remark in the same piece concerning the linguistic quality (or lack thereof) of the maiden issue of the SOBA *Newsletter* and are even considering it a sign of disloyalty on my part (as a well-known SOBAN), or a type of domestic-dirty-linen-washing in public. But, in this case, the linen had already been spread-out in public. The *Newsletter* in question was not for internal circulation only and, in fact, I bought my own copy in a very public place. Besides, I only pointed out the "dirty portions of the linen." I did not say or in any way imply that it was not good linen. The stories, features, poems and information in the SOBA *Newsletter* are quite good in spite of the purely linguistic and editorial shortcomings remarked. I did not set out to do a *Review* of the SOBA *Newsletter*.

Of course, one problem with Gobata is that even when he is taking aim at an elephant, he still has the penchant for hunting crickets and grasshoppers by the sides because the fans cherish the delicacies and may ignore or miss the elephant without them. In plain, simple language, I often use many heuristic devices or pep stories to make my pieces (which are no trifling matters) easily accessible and digestible. But my serious messages (which are never in doubt) should never be confused with any of my literary acrobatic stunts and calls for attention. Cameroonians, lend me your ears! A journey may be interesting and exciting, but it should not be confused with its destination. A journey cannot be so interesting and exciting that one would opt to remain on the road and never arrive. What does it profit a man (or even a woman) to taste the pepper and salt, *njanga* and *njangsa,* and then miss the meal itself with which they are seasoned?

Justified criticism is never and should not be considered a mark of disloyalty or enmity. On the contrary, severe but justified criticism is one of the best gifts you can give to or receive from those you truly love or are loved by.

Now, what concerns Pius Kwendi here is as follows: I sincerely congratulate him for being, so far, the third person ever to have taken up Gobata in writing, as I have never relented from urging my readers and especially critics to do. That is one of the foundation pillars of any liberal democratic society. Any idea that is put down in black and white takes a great risk: the risk of being objectively criticised and falsified. Decades from today, any objective enquirer will still be able to put Kwendi's rejoinder side by side with Gobata's piece and to make objective judgements and draw inescapable conclusions. To put anything critical in writing, is to take the risk of yourself being criticised and proved wrong, not to talk of the sundry purely physical risks from those who believe that a sharp cutlass is better than an argument or those who have mastered wielding the former but not the latter.

Nevertheless (and now I am qualifying my praise), I fail to see the pertinent point of Kwendi's rejoinder, although he quotes Gobata *in extenso.* He fails to show exactly where Gobata went wrong. His point seems to be the very general one that Gobata's praise of Ngwafor was qualified whereas he (Kwendi) would have preferred unqualified praise, a paradigmatic sample of which he gives (for Ngwafor's special attention?) in his second paragraph as follows: *."..one of our rare academic gems who, through sheer hard work and divine providence, became an epitome of perfection in the ivory tower."* This is exaggerated hyperbolic demagogic rhetoric. I would expect Ngwafor to be quite embarrassed at such incredible flattery.

Ngwafor is certainly a very conscientious hard-worker, but by no means a "rare academic gem" nor is he an "epitome of perfection" as the only being which be correctly so described is God. As for "divine providence," always take a deep breath whenever you hear that expression. In 1982 were we not all invincibly convinced that "divine providence" had sent us a saviour from tyrannic dictatorship? Had out collective critical consciousness not failed us at that epoch, would we not have realized that the divinity in question was the very dictator from whom we supposed ourselves saved?

Worse still, Kwendi imputes not only false illusions but motives of jealousy (certainly not the type of "practical jealousy" advocated by Ngwafor) and partisan sentiments on Gobata without the slightest attempt to substantiate any of such really very serious allegations. Turning Ngwafor into an "adversary" of Gobata (or vice versa), Kwendi takes strong exception to Gobata's description of Ngwafor as "loquacious." Is Kwendi against accurate or definite descriptions? Anybody who doesn't know Ngwafor personally can deduce his loquacity (or is it loquaciousness?) from the interview in the SOBA *Newsletter.*

So far, for what concerns Kwendi. I usually have *"preuves"* for all the claims I make in this column even if I don't immediately prove each of them to the point of saying *"quod erat demonstrandum."* But, if requested or challenged or, otherwise, put under appropriate pressure, I can produce such *"preuves"* with immediate effect, if not automatic alacrity.

I don't engage in polemics or run down people, nor do I criticise people with malice or for the mere fun of doing so, especially in this column; that is simply not in the Spirit of Gobata. But I never speak with my tongue in the cheek or with water in the mouth. I am capable of looking anybody in the eye and telling him/her what I truly and honestly think because there is never malice or any other unavowed motives, involved. I don't curry or expect *favours* from anybody nor do I fear being hated for speaking the truth, sticking to principles or arguing for justice and fair - play. I am an ardent advocate of meritocracy. I never hesitate to ask for what I believe I merit and to demand for my rights and deserts. Many times both my rights and meritocractic privileges and deserved prerogatives have been denied or wantonly trampled upon. But I am a patient long-term optimist who believes that the truth, justice as fairness and positive human values would eventually triumph over mediocrity, misuse of power in all its generic forms, and all shades of Machiavellian sophistries.

Written 18/09/96, published Tuesday, October 1, 1996.

9

A Rich Harvest of Peters by Paul

What's in a name? Very little. Especially Western names like Peter and Paul, Mary and Martha, which have no literal meaning but are simply convenient sounds used for purposes of personal identification. Almost any word or combination of words can serve as a name in the Western world. Some Western names can make you want to laugh. Some examples: Toogood, Badenough, Winterbottom, Head, Foot, Little, Littlehusband, Goodinbed, White, Black, Yellow, Green, Hammer, Bird, Angel, Satan, etc. African names usually have both literal meaning and significance but such meaning and significance are usually linked to an aspect of the autobiography of the name-giver rather than that of the name-bearer. A name is like a garment which anybody can put on, and you need to be very careful in drawing substantive inferences from the way a person is dressed, although the saying that "the apparel proclaims the wo(man)" is not without some foundation in truth.

Nevertheless, even though there may be nothing in a name, there is something quite uncannily remarkable about the psychology and behaviour, even about the physiology of certain name-bearers. For instance, I cannot remember ever coming across a "Gladys" who was not simply a complete package of beauty and vivaciousness. (Please, if you happen to bear "Gladys" don't rush over immediately after reading this, because you could jolly well turn out to be among the exceptions that prove the rule). There is a certain part of this country where no one would give his child the name "Hubert" (pronounced "Wuuber"). The very first person who bore that name there was a notorious thief and to refer to anybody as "a Wuuber" there is to call him a thief.

I have scarcely ever come across a "Martha" who was not the female equivalent of what among men is called a Casanova. Please, if you happen to be called Martha don't immediately rush for your pounding pestle and come after me. You may jolly well be one of the rare exceptions that prove the rule.

In lower primary school I used to be the errand boy of a certain Martha who hailed from one of the fraternal tributary neighbouring kingdoms and was in my village to attend the only Girls Primary School in the region. Martha used to send me with letters to several teachers and senior boys in the Boys School and always with firm instructions to hide it very well and not to let any other person see it. One day, a certain Christopher, a senior boy in my school, who hailed from the same place as Martha, called me and warned me that, since I had accepted to be Martha's "mail runner" to her numerous suitors, I should know that when they will "give her belle" I would be held responsible. I was very scared about this idea of being held responsible for her "belle" and had to completely change the trajectory of my normal way to school to avoid Martha and her love letters.

Another Martha of my own village, who was equally a female Casanova, used to write love letters to a boy only a few steps ahead of my age-grade, who used to show them to several other boys. Once Martha wrote; "My dear boy fren, I will come on Sunday and we do." This letter caused a lot of amusement among the boys because the "we do" was an inappropriate literal translation of the local dialect. Martha got the feed-back and, would you believe it?, was only worried that they were laughing at her for not knowing *lam barah* (the English language). So she went through her "'Michael West" Dictionary from cover to cover but could not find any suitable English word for "doing." Then she went to ask a senior colleague of hers, an *agaracha* and notorious female Casanova of her ilk, who, quite significantly, was also a Martha, what they call "doing" in English. No one knows what Martha (*trois*) told Martha (*deux*). But in her next love letter Martha wrote: "My dear boy fren, I will come again next Sunday and we fox again."

If I were asked to suggest the male counterpart of the female name Martha, I would unhesitatingly suggest "Paul," not necessarily because we say Peter and Paul the way we say Mary and Martha. However, I do know one or two Pauls who are the complete anti-thesis of Casanovas. But then again, incidentally, quite a good number of Pauls have been intimate friends of mine through the years and none of them would prove me wrong. Would any of those my very good personal friends bearing "Paul" like to step forward and prove me wrong?

As for Peter, whose full name is Simon Peter, though some people hang on to only one end and others to the other of it, I have never known a Peter in this our beloved triangle who was not either a remarkable rascal as a boy or a fanatical supporter of his Excellency Paul Biya as a man, or both of the above. From West Cameroon, in particular, his Excellency Paul has had an abundantly rich harvest of Peters, remarkably staunch supporters or, at least, professors of his "New Deal" theosophy, since the democratic struggle began in this country. There is no need reading their roll call again. You know all of them thoroughly well. Let us only note here that the newly appointed Prime Minister (and Head of Government?) is a Peter replacing a Simon, thanks to a mere head shake of Paul's.

What difference does it make when a crow replaces a raven? Without having answered such a question, I am quite surprised at the excitement and euphoria that the recent (should I say cabinet reshuffle?) has caused. But how can I say cabinet reshuffle? A Head of Government reshuffles his cabinet. If, for any justifiable reason, the Head of Government has to fall, his entire cabinet goes down with him. A general election is then held and a new Head elected or appointed to form a new government. What did the previous PM and Head of Government do wrong to merit a sack? Anyway, not to worry. Would he not, as usual, be called to another corner of the table? To appoint a Head of Government and also his cabinet for him clearly shows that the real Head of Government is someone else who can sack both the supposed Head and part or whole of his supposed government at will. This is like the Head Boy or Senior Prefect in the secondary school where there is no doubt that power and authority lie but with the principal. There is nothing particularly inconsistent in such a system but it should not be confused with democracy, backward or advanced. Such a political system is properly and accurately described as a monarchic autocracy. Since 1990, our autocratic monarchy is still frantically jogging on the same spot while mouthing democratic verbiage.

People have been celebrating, as usual, whereas maybe they should really start weeping for the plantations and other natural resources of southern Southern Cameroons. After a bottle too many, some have even been boasting loudly: "At last we have really arrived! We will really show those people. Let them all go and die of jealousy.

Nonsense! It is now our turn" Who are the "we" here? Do they realise that a royal head that shakes once could shake once again? In any case, let no one forget that the greatest beneficiaries of the removal of the Honourable Simon Achidi Achu, MP, PM and Head of Government, would be his kith and kin of Santa, who may at last find concord and harmony amongst themselves again. And, were it not that there are still many other high-flight Northwesterners in government, with the prerogative of ordering a truck-load of gendarmes at any time to go and maintain *"l'ordre publique"* anywhere, we might even have been sure that the North West "tribal wars" would dramatically subside. Truly I tell you, blessed are those communities which have never had a minister or governmental big man, for they would surely have learnt self-reliance which alone can transform a people's life for the better and make lasting peace and harmony theirs. No community can really prosper out of "eating *awuuf"* from public coffers.

As for Honourable Peter Mafany Musonge, the new PM and Head of Government, we should not pre-judge him. For, even though there is no identifiable difference between a crow and a raven, the crow can fly in a straighter line than a raven, if it so chooses. But, were I to suggest, I would say that he should leave the economy alone. Paul himself has been on that for a decade without any results. Let him tackle officialised corruption without whose eradication the economy will never improve. Simple things like this thirty percent affair at the public treasuries; regular and systematic extortion from motorists by members of the armed forces; organised robbery at the ports; this 650.000 francs business for admission into ENS etc. etc.

Written 23/09/96, published Tuesday. October 22, 1996.

10

The Collapse of the French Empire in Africa

The French have received more than a fair share of my critical attention since 1990. I have voluntarily and freely given the French very important strategic advice of the type I also gave His Excellency Paul Biya, particularly in 1990. Elsewhere such advice would have been given under secret cover and I would have been called an "'expert consultant'" and paid heavily. But in both cases (can a pupil be expected to do better than his teacher or a disciple better than his master?) my valuable free strategic advice was not only completely ignored but treated with disdain as can be clearly seen from the seizure and continuous detention of *The Past Tense of Shit (Book One)*. By the way, they succeeded in seizing and detaining (or destroying?) the book, but can they also succeed in seizing and detaining or destroying its contents? The answer is blowing in the wind.

By the way again, after a series of procedural false starts, *Book Two of the Past Tense*, entitled *I SPIT ON THEIR GRAVES,* with a *Foreword* by Ni John Fru Ndi and an *Epilogue* by Simon Munzu has finally been published by an American publisher. Copies should reach Cameroon in the coming weeks. Please, book for your copy with the nearest CamPost person or dépot to you. As democratisation has probably made some progress since 1993, we shall surely attempt to arrange a launching ceremony for the book (backed by CRTV publicity) when it arrives here, at the Yaounde Municipal Town Hall, among other places.

We were talking about the collapse of the French Empire in Africa. The French Empire in Africa is fast collapsing. From a distance I had sighted this approaching collapse and attempted (unsuccessfully) to advise the French in their own self-interest that their best bet lay in siding with the majoritarian masses and genuinely and honestly supporting democratisation in Africa rather than in their continued propping-up and support of rapacious dictators and repressive regimes. Even from the present very close quarters, some people are still unable to see the fast-approaching collapse of the French Empire in Africa. Myopia. Some Cameroonians are still inseparable from their French suits and get overly excited over rumours of the type "The French have already chosen Biya's successor for 1997."

Read *Book Two of the Past Tense*. The French can never complain of being ignored or treated with levity in that book. When they went to the *Francophonie* summit in Mauritius in 1993 and solemnly declared that the main purpose of that body was to combat "Anglo-Saxon cultural imperialism" did I not describe the declaration as "Quixotic" and ask what they thought would happen were the Anglo-Saxon world to retaliate in self-defence? The Anglo-Saxon world has never bothered to react but shortly after the Mauritius summit, Rwanda, a Francophonie country, declared for English in preference to French as its "national language." Recently, Algeria, another Francophonie country; where, since the fifties, French neo-colonialism has murdered thousands of people and provoked genocidal civil strife to protect French interests, has declared English its *first* national language and relegated French to second place. In France itself, films, advertisements and music in English have been proscribed from all public media. But this has only helped to intensify their attraction for young French people.

Elsewhere I have drawn the contrasts between the French and their other comrades in (neo-)colonialism, in their various styles and *modus operandi*. I need not dwell on that again here. But do you think that the gains of English over French are because English in itself is in any way better than French? It is a fact, as I have remarked before, that French as a language, is smoother on the lips and sweeter in the ear than English. That is why, when it comes to *talking*, francophones will always out-talk Anglophones any day, anywhere. And, moreover, they always supplement their very fine talking with frantic manual gestures and bodily postures reminiscent of any conductor of a classical orchestra. Should the unusual happen and you outclass a francophone in sheer talking, he would usually resort to *"des instructions d'en haut"* to silence you and win what he had lost in a fair talking combat. For culture and leisure, for joking and empty rhetoric, for amorous canticles, love lullabies and sweet nothings, the French language has no rival. But for serious things like science and technology, business and commerce, academic research and communication, etc you have to turn to English, whether you like it or not.

Do you think that those Francophone Cameroonians who have been rushing to the British Council, American Cultural Centre, the Pilot Centre and those Francophone parents who have flooded the Yaounde PNEU nursery and primary school with their kids don't know what they are doing? By 1982, Bernard Fonlon, the architect and ideologist of Cameroon's policy of bilingualism, had changed his mind under pragmatic imperatives and advocated that English should be Cameroon's *first* national official language. There is stiff official resistance to this suggestion but, on the ground itself, it is daily becoming a *de facto* reality. The concerted effort to destroy the GCE system of examination and, by extension, the entire "Anglo-Saxon' system of education in Cameroon, is the centre piece of the resistance. This misguided offensive would celebrate a major victory the day all Cameroonians speak English like their Honourable Excellencies, Mbella Mbappe and Frederic Kodock. Those two really deserve national awards for boldly and shamelessly bulldozing their way, whenever the need arises, through English, without any fear or favour.

Both the French language and the French Empire in Africa are fighting battles which have been lost in advance. More Francophone African countries are going to opt for English in preference to French as a pragmatic *desideratum* in the coming years. Quote me! French will, of course, continue to be widely used in those domains, like the ones I have delineated above, where it is appropriate and unrivalled. As genuine democratic systems slowly replace French-imposed dictatorships all over Africa, the French Empire in Africa will simply pale out of existence. I know some people would never believe me until 1999 when the effects of the European Common Currency would start to be felt in Francophone Africa. It is then that it would be clear to everybody that an African Common Market and Currency are inevitable for our survival. For those who understand and believe me, we can together already spit in advance on the grave of the French Empire in Africa.

Written 06/10/96, published Tuesday, October 29, 1996.

11

Between Mvondo and Mvodo; The Emergence of Victor Ayissi

Honourable Victor Ayissi Mvodo, an erstwhile Minister under Ahidjo's dictatorship, has emerged from the wings, as it were, and announced his candidature for the up-coming (1997) presidential elections, through the pages of the French language weekly *La Nouvelle Expression* (NO. 352, 15 October 1996). This is a very significant event in the democratisation struggle in Cameroon which must be put into proper perspective.

In thus coming out from the wings and openly avowing his presidential ambition, Victor Ayissi Mvodo counterposes himself, first and foremost, against his *countriman*, Biya Bi Mvondo Paul. The first reaction of some people might be to wonder what the difference is between Mvodo and Mvondo and many may easily assimilate it to the difference between a raven and a crow. Would choosing between Mvodo and Mvondo be like choosing between a rock and a hard place, between the devil and the deep blue sea?

Be that as it may, I believe, that that small letter "n" could make all the difference. The "Ayissi factor" could change the course of our political history. Had this factor emerged during, before or after the 1992 presidential elections, we might all have been spared the anguish of the past four years. Nevertheless, as they say, *better late than never*.

The importance of Ayissi's challenge, if it is sustained, is that it will break the *very* dangerous myth that the Centre-South-East of Cameroon is a homogeneous single political entity, divinely carved out and reserved for Biya Bi Mvondo, a sacred and sacrosanct area where no one dares to campaign except for Biya and the CPDM. This myth, which has been sustained by civil administrators and members of the armed forces, has greatly helped in creating the impression that our democratisation struggle and politics in general has not yet transcended tribalism. Our national politics and consciousness transcended tribalism and parochialism a long time ago with the rise of Ni John Fru Ndi, although the present dictatorship has found it very expedient to encourage and use tribalism in its frantic determination to hang on to the rafters of illegitimate and unpopular power.

It is, as yet unclear from which political party platform Ayissi Mvodo intends to canvas his 1997 presidential bid. Although he himself claims to be a member of the CPDM party, stalwarts of that party, such as Albert Dzongang, in the same edition of *La Nouvelle Expression,* would seem to cast doubt on that claim. We note in passing that, since the advent of multi-parties in this country, all civil servants, public officials and government employees are presumed, as by obligation, to belong to the CPDM.

Hence, they are usually called upon at any time, by radio announcements, without any prior consultation, to go on campaign trips for the party. The silent majority, that is, all those who are not vocal members of any of the opposition parties are also presumed to be members of the CPDM as can be clearly seen from the fact that in places where no election takes place, such as during the last municipals, the CPDM is invariably declared the winner.

Reading through Ayissi Mvodo's interview, I have the impression that he must be one of those progressives, like Simon Munzu, who attempted unsuccessfully to democratise the CPDM. What I cannot, however, understand is why he has been so quiet up till now and how he could have managed to maintain his silence in the face of, say, the outrages of 1992 and 1993. The resilience of dictatorship in Cameroon is directly related to the failure to democratise the CNU alias CPDM.

As someone who is, no doubt, greatly respected by His Excellency Paul Biya, imagine what might have happened had Ayissi Mvodo spoken out loudly and clearly at the crucial moments of our democratisation struggle. You may be wondering how I managed to know that Paul Biya greatly respects Ayissi Mvodo. Easy. Mvodo is alleged to have once, in the presence of Ahidjo, given Bi Mvondo, then Prime Minister, a dirty slap. Ayissi was even asked to confirm or deny this widely told story during the interview with *La Nouvelle Expression*. Very significantly, he answered that, since he was never sanctioned for the slap either by Ahidjo or Biya himself, as President and Prime Minister, respectively, nor was he ever taken to court, that Paul Biya should be the one to be asked to confirm or deny the fact. You cannot help respecting someone who can give you a dirty slap and get away with it, especially if the person in question is, in any sense, a subordinate of yours. It is claimed that His Excellency has never been seen in such a state of panic as when he learned that Ayissi was determined to challenge him. So, evidently, had Ayissi stuck out his neck and, maybe, issued another sound slap around the early nineties, when the democratisation struggle gathered momentum. Biya might never have persisted, against all honest advice, in continuing with dictatorship under the guise of an "advanced democracy" and would, in the contrary case, certainly have returned the "stolen victory" of the 1992 elections to the rightful owner.

In spite of the efforts of his hand-picked *nchindas,* the fon of Fons is so unpopular that it would be expecting a miracle to think that he could conceivably win any free and fair election in Cameroon today, as yesterday. I recently attended one of these public ceremonies which have nothing to do with politics but where many of the shit-shiners and panel-beaters of the regime were heavily involved as speakers. Every time someone demagogically mentioned him… "Eh, as his Excellency who incarnates this and that has always said…" there was loud spontaneous booing from the crowd. Do these fellows ever honestly report these things back to their master? The answer is blowing in the wind.

The most reasonable and honourable path for Ayissi Mvodo is to sustain his bid for the CPDM nomination as presidential candidate for 1997 during the CPDM congress already announced for next month. If he succeeds in his bid, it would be a great victory for the democratic struggle in this country. It would also improve the chances of the CPDM in any (free and fair!) elections although the party has done itself so much damage that it would be miraculous for it to actually win any free and fair election in the foreseeable future. But it would also be miraculous if Ayissi Mvodo were to succeed in getting his party's nomination, given that everything that has been done in this country since 1992 - from attempts at a tailor-made constitution through the imposition of "government delegates" on opposition urban councils to reshufflement of the cabinet - has all been geared towards maintaining the incumbent, by hook or crook, on his monarchic throne.

Should Ayissi Mvodo fail in his bid, then he could possibly be a valuable asset to existing opposition parties, depending on how many people, from his present party or otherwise, are willing and ready to stand behind him and move with him. DEMOCRACY IS A GAME OF NUMBERS! In this case, it is to be hoped that Ayissi Mvodo would get in touch with the other opposition leaders, who are already trying to work out some common strategies and alliances for the coming elections. Some people have been whispering around that Ayissi Mvodo is France's choice as Biya's successor. This is very foolish talk and I am happy that he himself has given no cause to make such a supposition credible. If it were true, it would do him great political damage. We have not been struggling to deny dictatorship to Cameroonians so that France may continue to be the only dictator on our political scene. French neo-colonialism in Africa is on its way out and the French Empire in Africa is on the brink of collapse. The days of France's hand-picked dictators in Africa are over. France's best interest in Africa now lies in supporting *genuine* democratic systems and structures. Quote me!

The chief importance of Victor Ayissi Mvodo's emergence and declaration of presidential ambition is in its frontal challenge of the Biya dynasty. But it is to be hoped that it would not provoke a spate of *JE SERAI CANDIDAT* from other ambitious Cameroonians. Democracy is not a one-man show. One doesn't enter the democratic political game from the summit. With good and strong followers, even a very weak person can lead well. This time around, let us hear but from the political parties. And, if the opposition parties can learn lessons from their past errors, they should work out their strategies and agreements very well in silence before publicizing them. We earnestly hope that there will be no jokers and jesters on the scene this time around.

Written 18/10/96, published Tuesday, November 5, 1996.

12

Corruption Fights Cameroon

There is a famous Nigerian cartoonist named Josy Ajiboye who, for decades, has been cartooning regularly for the *Sunday Times of Nigeria.* Many people find it hard to miss an issue of the *Sunday Times of Nigeria,* not because of its news content, stories and write-ups, but because of the little front page corner reserved for Ajiboye's Sunday cartoon. Some of Josy Ajiboye's cartoons can make you laugh until you cry. In 1982 or thereabouts one appeared with the caption CORRUPTION FIGHTS NIGERIA. The cartoon was a boxing ring in which a really frightful "Goliath" named Corruption was warming up and waiting for the bell to take on a malnourished and rickety-looking "David" named Nigeria. Even the referee was looking quite frightened. This cartoon appeared at a time when Nigeria's kleptocratic leaders were making a lot of noise all over the place about Nigeria fighting corruption. With a simple cartoon, Ajiboye said all that needed to be said about the bold pretence of the shameless kleptocrats: "Nigeria" was not fighting any corruption: it was corruption fighting Nigeria. That cartoon, so apt for Nigeria in 1982, is even apter (if you would permit) for Cameroon in 1996.

Today, indomitable corruption is fighting Cameroon. For over a decade now the vampires have been dancing their macabre dance (ask the playwright, Bole Butake). But, instead of caging them and taking them, in disgrace, to the market-place, the rest of us have instead joined in the dance, each at his/her own pace and tempo, at all levels and sectors of our national life. The rhythm of the vampires has become the life beat to which every Cameroonian dances, willy-nilly. It is amazing that some Cameroonians were surprised, (some even offended!), by a recent American survey which listed Cameroon among the seven most corrupt countries on earth.

In Cameroon corruption hits you on the face, like a trained boxer's punch, the moment you set foot on Cameroon territory, whether via land, sea or air. The myriad uniformed officers who perform entry formalities as well as those who stand idly on the roads (you call this a road?) are all shameless extortionists. This is a country where you can watch your own car being off-loaded from the ship at the port and, before you finish stamping your certificate of ownership in the nearby office, it would have been emptied of all its contents and stripped of all strippable parts, right there inside the fenced port under the idle gaze of customs officers, gendarmes and police officers. You would be told that if you return there regularly you might be lucky to buy your own very missing property at a "good price."

If you use the public means of transportation, whether intra or inter any of our cities provinces or regions, you would surely think that the only normal and regular function of our armed forces is controlling transportation vehicles. In any case, there is nothing else they seem to do with such enthusiasm and punctuality as stopping vehicles on the road. You see them there, no matter how early in the morning or late at night, under the sun or in the rain. They would then demand the "pieces de vehicule" and start walking towards the back of the car where the driver of the vehicle would follow them, quickly give some money and promptly regain the documents. If on checking "cartes d'idenitités" you happen not to have yours, they would order the driver to put down your bag and start handcuffing you saying that you are a *"Biafrais."* But when a bill changes hands, you would be released without any further ado.

The malady has spread to and engulfed all sections and aspects of our public life. In our educational institutions today students pay raw cash to the teachers or administrators to pass their exams. Go and have a chat with, say, the Rector of the University of Yaounde I and you wouldn't believe the corrupt practices that have been going *on* there with the culpable connivance of those in charge. At our public hospitals today, after paying all the usual fees, patients have to put a two thousand francs bill inside their "carnet" before it is passed on to the doctor, or else s/he would not consult. If an injection is prescribed, 500 francs would have to be paid to the nurse for it to be administered. A young doctor who confirmed this to me recently argued that it is justifiable because the police take money on the roads and this is the only way medical personnel can also survive. The 30% business at the public treasuries is no longer news to anybody. But every day new methods of fraud are invented every where. For submitting your tax declaration forms this year, you were required to give a photocopy each of the national identities of yourself and your wife and the sum of 3000 francs in cash. What has the national identity card got to do with tax declaration and what is the 3000 francs for? The answers are blowing in the wind.

There is one of these *yeye* tertiary institutions of higher learning where prospective students usually pay unbelievable sums of money to get admitted because they know that on graduation they would acquire the license to retail examination marks to secondary school students.

For this reason, graduation from this institution is usually a very grand affair during which the graduands wear some funny-looking "academic dress." Now, would you believe that this dress, which costs a fortune, is exclusively supplied by the Director of the said *yeye* institution himself? In any decent country it would be a public scandal if even a remote relation of his were to be given such a contract. But Cameroonians seem to have taken all these malpractices as rather in the normal order of things.

But how did we get here? Your guess is as good as mine. I had once pointed out that it is extremely dangerous for the moral health of our society to allow the practice whereby people bribe their way into *Ecole de Police*, *CUSS*, *ENAM*, *Ecole de Poste*, *ENS*, *IRIC*, *ASMAC*, *INJS*, etc. These are the people who would be responsible for probity and moral sanity in society. So how can they be expected to fulfil this role if they started their career on a fraudulent note?

Cameroonians have become completely unshockable by fraud and corruption because large-scale fraud and corruption at the highest rungs of the state have gone without any sanction. Recall the ruination of the Marketing Board, CAMBANK, the Messi Messi affair, the CELUCAM scandal etc, etc. We have all quickly forgotten these things as if they had never happened. Our shockability before such moral scandals and outrageous frauds (or is it fraudulent outrages?) is what will completely destroy us as a people unless we start <u>NOW</u> to collectively reconscientize ourselves. Our moral crisis is much more dangerous than the economic crisis and dictatorship that have been menacing us in the last ten years. There can be a decent dictatorship and there are very decent poor nations and peoples. But a morally bankrupt people or nation is indeed without any glimmer of hope.

Written 28/10/96, published Tuesday, November 12, 1996

13

Rumours of Dangerous Manoeuvres and Machinations

Although we have continued saying that *"Le Cameroun c'est le Cameroun"* and sometimes, with apparent justification, we need to remind ourselves constantly that le Cameroun could cease to be le Cameroun at any time, if we are not careful. I am told that when Omar Bongo, the "Doe," alias sit-tight dictator of Gabon, was once asked what he would like to be, were it possible for him to come back to the world again after death, he answered, without any hesitation, that he would like to come back as the President of Cameroon! His reason for this very interesting answer was that a country where a 70% general salary cut could be carried out on the eve of a 100% devaluation of the currency without as much as a token resistance from the population must be a paradise to govern. So Bongo has been greatly envious of his brother and comrade-in-dictatorship, Paul Biya of Cameroon.

It is, of course, significantly interesting that His Excellency Omar Bongo, like ours truly, is incapable of thinking of himself as anything other than a President. That is why he immediately (mis)understood the question as to what, if given the chance, he would like to come back to life as, to mean "as President of which other country?!" Very interesting and also significant. But let us not hunt for grasshoppers yet with the feet.

Cameroonians are, indeed, a very docile lot. Docility is sometimes an advantage, a virtue, but most times, it is a vice, a great handicap in life. Our docility might have helped us to avoid upheavals and civil war up to the present, but that may only have prepared us for more dangerous upheavals and civil war in future. «He who fights and runs away from the fight lives to fight another day." We may ignore the fact, but, potentially, Cameroon has got all it takes to out-Rwanda Rwanda and to out-Burundi Burundi. Let us not deceive ourselves now and regret later. The problem of Southern Cameroons which the powers that be have always tried to sweep under the carpet is only lying low at the moment, it has not gone away. And it will never go away until it is squarely and fairly faced. The problem of the "stolen victory" and subverted general will of 1992 has been allowed to go to rest only because of the hope of redress and vindication in 1997.

So, rumours that the regime in power is preparing to wangle through parliament legislation that would exclude, *ex hypothesi*, the one person and party most capable of winning a land-slide victory in any free and fair elections should be of grave concern to all Cameroonians who love this country and know where their own best personal interest lies. Given the history of rumours of this nature in this country, no one should wait for confirmation or disconfirmation before reacting. If we allow ourselves to be manoeuvred into going into the coming elections with unfair or unclear rules and/or without an independent and transparently fair umpire, we are surely courting civil war that would make Rwanda and Burundi look like children playing in the courtyard. Fraud is something that we should never ever tolerate in elections in this country again, including fraud before the elections such as in unfair rules and fraud after the elections such as in finding a pretext to impose the loser as the winner (recall the 1992 lame excuse of the Supreme Court and the 1996 imposition of "government delegates" on opposition urban councils).

As I am writing this, the CRTV is celebrating the rapacious plunder of the last 14 years under the very ironic title of **LIBERTY WEEK!** When shall we be liberated from the iron grip of our incumbent kleptocratic dictatorship? Any foreign observer could surely conclude that Cameroonians have a very bizzare sense of humour. Would you be surprised if their autocratic Excellencies, Sese Seko Mobutu of Zaire and Gnasingbe Eyadema of Togo, also organise, each in his own turn, a Liberty Week, to celebrate their invention and bequeathal of democracy to their respective peoples?

The very recent incarceration of Pius Njawe shows that very little, if anything at all, has changed in this country since 1990 when the democratic struggle was launched. And, if we do not quickly regain the fiery fervour and enthusiasm, the spirit of endurance and sacrifice of 1990/91, then we should be ready for unpleasant surprises such as having to continue enduring the smell of rotten meat for another seven years. Let those who are not horrified and terrified by such a prospect raise their hands and step forward to be recognised.

It is very important that we should collectively tackle all the manoeuvres and machinations of the incumbent dictatorship under the guise of democracy, promptly, as and when they occur, instead of waiting to cry over spilt milk again in the end. A fool at forty is a fool forever and a fool for the second time, over the same matter, is also a fool forever. Those who accepted palm oil during the last Municipal Elections and cast their vote for dictatorship to continue under the garb of verbal democracy should look at their mouths carefully on the mirror whether they will still see any traces of the oil they ate on their lips. Are they any better off than those of us who did not eat any *awuuf* oil? The answer is blowing in the wind.

No Cameroonian, both among the silent masses and among the noisy few who think democracy is simply a matter of waking up from your comfortable bed and declaring *"JE SERAI CANDIDAT,"* can pretend not to know how and under whose leadership we can achieve genuine democracy in Cameroon next year. If we fail again to do so, we deserve whatever fate awaits us as a consequence.

Written 06/11/96, published Tuesday, November 19, 1996.

14

Politics of Back Scratching

It is Honourable (?) Simon Achidi Achu, ex-this and that, who is generally credited with the copyright of the political theory of back-scratching. I don't know if Achidi Achu is the actual originator of this theory, but he is certainly its clearest enunciator and most ardent exponent. He adumbrated this very interesting theory shortly after he was appointed Prime Minister and supposed Head of Government at a time that the country was on the verge of a popular revolt, spear-headed by the Northwest Province, his political base, against repressive dictatorship. Achidi Achu's main assignment as PM was to help His Excellency Paul Biya remain on his monarchical throne for the following five years. He tackled his assignment with remarkable promptitude, originality, deftness and alacrity. Combining stick and carrot strategies, he soon got the restless and restive populations to give up their determination to save themselves from tyrannic rule. He sent gendarmes to the most stubborn areas to light fires for naked (if you understand) women to jump over while elsewhere beer bottles were pushed up the secret crevices of those the red berets had exhausted themselves raping. Bundles of money were carelessly flung at traditional rulers as if money were not a scarce commodity.

Achidi Achu charmed the crowds with his down-to-earth rhetoric:

"Politics na njangi; you scratch my back I scratch your own! You yip me today I yip you tomorrow. Na Mr. Paul Biya send me make I salute una."

When Achidi Achu was sacked as PM after having achieved all his master's aims, someone remarked:

"You see this man now. He bin say make we drink njangi and say na him go first chop njangi. He say if we yip him today he go yip we tomorrow, Nobi na we don loss? Nobi na say he don chop we money so? As dem don

sack he for work so how he go manage yip we again
tomorrow? De man get sense pass mark. Small time he
fit come say make we start anoda different njangi again
and say na him go first chop njangi again. De man get
sense, but we too no go fool again."

What would never have occurred to me is that Honourable Peter
Mafany Musonge, Achidi Achu's technocratic successor in office,
is also an ardent catechist of this Achidian political doctrine. Since
his appointment we had come to regard Honourable Musonge as
one of those anomalous oddities in the Biya regime, that is, an
honest, straightforward and capable simple citizen with no history
of or tendency towards trickery and crockery who, for quite
unfathomable reasons, the big boss of us all now sees as the
pragmatic linchpin, the means to the end of achieving his most
immediate aims, whatever these may be. But Honourable Musonge
frankly surprised me by expressing the back-scratching *philofolly* not
only with remarkable eloquence but apparent conviction, at Buea,
during the opening of his maiden visit as PM to his natal Province.
According to him, the post of Prime Minister is a highly coveted
one and, by appointing him, a son of the South West, to that post,
the President, Mr. Biya, was scratching the back of the people of
the South West. So they should not forget to scratch Biya's back in
return. Politics na Njangi. Abi?

The problem with this back-scratching *philofolly*, as I see it, is as
follows: By appointing Peter Mafany Musonge as Prime Minister,
in what sense can it be said that Paul Biya is scratching the back of
the people of the South West Province to warrant reciprocal back-
scratching from them? Do all Southwesterners feed on Musonge's
dining table? Are Southwesterners not being offered a euphoric
illusion in exchange for which they are expected to neglect saving
themselves and the rest of Cameroonians from the repressive
dictatorship and rapacious pillage (or is it pillageous rape?) and
plunder of the past one and a half decades?

But, if in some sense that I have failed to understand,
Southwesterners can truly claim that their backs have been
"scratched" in the appointment of Honourable Musonge, then the

question is: What reason would the people of the other nine provinces, whose backs have not been similarly "scratched," have for supporting Mr. Biya and his regime?

We ought to demand good government, not back-scratching. The back-scratching *Philofolly* is what has led to the incredible rape, pillage and plunder of this country, to the benefit of a handful of crooks. Politics may be about *interests*, but it is not a matter of crudely distributing raw cash or rice and palm oil around. A bridge constructed over a river or a kilometre of road tarred is to everybody's interest but to no particular person's benefit. A million francs given to a "chef traditionnel" is to his personal benefit unless he is an extraordinary philanthropist to use it in financing a community project.

There is an elderly professor whom I used to admire and respect. Between the short time that I took my meditative retreat and my return, he had transformed into a staunch "Newdealer," going on CPDM missions and campaigns with avid alacrity. When I asked what was happening, I was told that he said government was owing him too much money and the only way he could recover part of it was to join "them." Quite interestingly, many people consider his action quite a wise move. It may be *clever* but it is not *wise*. Quote me. Politics is not about these kinds of narrow, parochial, personal interests.

Politics is also about *performance*. When I claim that, if the forthcoming elections are *free and fair*, the New Deal regime would not only lose but lose resoundingly with a landslide failure, it is simply on the basis of its proven performance (or lack thereof). I have drawn the balance sheet and provided the "preuves" many times before. There have been anomalous oddities, veritable misfits, within the New Deal -individuals who attempted swimming against the strong current of its accumulated *philofollies* and catastrophic practices. People like Sanda Oumarou and Garga Haman Adji (there are no *et ceteras*) who stood head and shoulders above the normative mediocrity, depravity and kleptocracy.

One such anomaly presently in the New Deal regime is Mr. Akame Mfoumou, Minister of Finance. Everybody is applauding what Akame Mfoumou has been attempting to do since his arrival at the Finance ministry, because there is nothing so convincing as performative action. Akame Mfoumou is trying to dismantle a blood-sucking corrupt mafia in his new ministry which, for years, has operated with quasi-official connivance. Akame Mfoumou has simply got down to work; no demagogy about what the President of the Republic who incarnates this and that has always said or stood for. By trying to institute a fair and objective procedure for the payment of treasury vouchers, Akame Mfoumou is not doing any one person or group of persons a favour. He is not scratching any person's back. He is doing something that is in the interest of all Cameroonians, of any Cameroonian, irrespective of their individuating and particularising characteristics. This is not like flamboyantly handing out sacks of stolen rice and embezzled palm oil.

A young military officer of Northwest origin told me (long before the recent cabinet reshuffle) that Akame Mfoumou cannot stand corruption; that he successfully fought against and dismantled a corrupt and powerful mafia in the Ministry of Defence, especially at the Military Academy. «From their fruits we shall know them», Dispositionally and perfomatively, Akame Mfoumou does <u>not</u> belong to the New Deal pack. Why can the New Deal not propose someone like that as its Presidential Candidate for 1997? The answer is blowing in the wind.

Written 10/11/96, published Tuesday, November 26, 1996.

15

For the Attention of All Potential Ethnic Cleansers

Ethnic cleansing is a truly horrible idea that had its origin, birth and flowering in Europe, especially in Nazi Germany. It is closely connected with and is, in fact, a direct consequence of ideas about genetic superiority and attendant racism. Under the Nazis, this configuration of ideas and attitudes led to the genocidal massacre of over 6 million Jews around the time of the Second World War, only half a century ago. The war traumatised Europe and shocked the conscience of the entire world. But ethnic cleansing survived the war and has recently manifested itself spectacularly in Bosnia, Chechnya, etc. It has been exported to Africa by European neo-colonialism and has demonstrated its pernicious efficacy in Rwanda and Burundi.

Africa is the most diverse continent, ethnically and otherwise and, before the European intervention and colonisation, African tribes and ethnic groups took one another simply for granted, although tribal tensions, conflicts and. occasionally, war have never been completely absent at any historical epoch. But such conflicts or wars were usually ritually settled in a manner and context which clearly took for granted *the right* of all the conflicting or warring parties *to exist*. Even throughout the period of European colonisation, African tribes which were artificially bonded together at the Berlin Conference of 1884 for the convenience of the European powers coexisted remarkably harmoniously. Genocidal conflicts of the scale of Rwanda and Burundi are a creation of neo-colonialism, which, in order to continue exploitation of the continent as if colonialism had never ended, has found it necessary to play one group of Africans against another. This strategy of predators unwilling to give up their predatory activities has been rendered more dangerous by the free supply of sophisticated weapons. As long as any group of people possess or (especially) monopolise weapons which their "enemies," ""opponents" or "rivals" do not have, for so long will their aggressive instincts and predatory dispositions control their rationality.

Some form or other of rivalry between distinct groups of people or human communities is almost inevitable. If such rivalry is based on some objectively respectable considerations or criteria, it can be a very healthy thing for society as a whole. But, as a matter of fact, identifiable groups of people have always tended to misuse their power, be this political, economic, military or numerical. That is why it is very important that even genuine *democracy* should have *meritocracy* as an inseparable and indispensable companion. Outside a meritocratic framework, people who possess any of the powers mentioned above would always want to use unfair means to gain advantages over the others. And, if they should succeed in monopolising all the powers, they cannot help arrogating to themselves the prerogative to decide who would live and who would die.

Among extreme right-wing whites, no secret is made of the fact that the African continent (minus its people) is considered as a continent on reserve just in case the effects of industrialisation eventually make the western world uninhabitable. For sometime the neutron bomb had a certain fascination because of tins. But more recently, it has appeared that if the western world or certain powerful segments thereof wanted to empty the African continent of its human contents they wouldn't need to do more than instigate hatred amongst the various different groups of people and then supply them abundantly with dangerous weapons. Rwanda and Burundi are very promising initial experiments in this regard.

In Cameroon, the emergence of "autochthones-alogènes" vocabulary and rhetoric was the first step towards searching for a viable formula by which the Rwanda scenario could be easily recreated in Cameroon if (some) Cameroonians continued attempting to take their destiny firmly into their own hands. But a little reflection and vicarious historical experience clearly shows that, if we allow ourselves to be led down that path, there would be no victors at the end of the day and we would all be equally vanquished.

Because of the seriousness of this matter, there is a little story carried in some newspapers of last week that should not be passed over in silence or even left to await further confirmatory investigations. No University worth its salt would admit less academically qualified candidates in place of their betters. But, did the University of Yaounde I go even further to reject highly qualified candidates on account of their provinces of origin and to admit their academic inferiors? My dear Sirs, has the ethnic cleansing begun?

Written 04/12/96, published Tuesday, December 24, 1996.

16

Independent Electoral Commission, an Absolute Necessity

With the mandate of our first supposedly democratically elected parliament coming to an end, Cameroonians have one rare opportunity again to set this country on the firm path of democracy, responsible government, peace and prosperity. The parliament whose life-span is ending might be described as multi-party or pluralist but not as democratic. In fact, it only helped to create the illusion, especially for outsiders, that our dictatorship had been transformed into a democracy. This outgoing parliament started its term on the rebound from the denial and brutal suppression of the popular demand for a Sovereign National Conference (SNC) which would have put this country on the firm path of genuine democracy. Similarly, the parliament has ended its term on the crest of the stubborn denial of another reasonable popular demand – the creation of an Independent Electoral Commission (IEC).

Quite interestingly, these parliamentarians who helped in no small way to give our dictatorship the semblance of a democracy, in exchange for personal gains within a mutual back-scratching philofolly, wanted their mandate prolonged by presidential decree. Some people are even crediting our dictatorship for the failure of their diabolic plan and equating it with the failure of the bill introduced by the UNDP for an Autonomous Electoral Commission (AEC). Those who think that the failure of both projects shows fairness, impartiality and even-handedness have failed to see that the first project was a call for the violation of the Constitution while the second sought to enhance the democratic nature of the Constitution.

An Independent Electoral Commission remains an absolute necessity, a foundational pillar of genuine and long-lasting democracy, not only in Cameroon but anywhere else in the world. By the way, I tried unsuccessfully to get in touch with the UNDP to suggest that they should amend the title of their proposed bill from "Autonomous Electoral Commission" to "Independent Electoral Commission." An "autonomous" commission would be one that makes its own laws and I don't think we want to create a commission that would be a law-giver unto itself. What we need is a commission that works within terms of reference laid down by law but that is "independent" of any executive control or manipulation. I know that what the UNDP draftsmen had foremost in their minds was the idea of financial autonomy of the body but such financial autonomy is already part, in fact, a condition, of its independence and it is misleading and inappropriate to describe the whole body as "autonomous" because of this.

I am making this suggestion because I know that, sooner or later, as we inch our way painfully towards genuine democracy, we will have to have an Independent Electoral Commission. I might even go as far as predicting that it would be created by the new parliament after the parliamentary elections in March 1997. That the ruling CPDM will lose the forthcoming elections with a landslide is not a matter of doubt to any well-informed person. But this does not mean that the CPDM may not win future elections, depending on the performance and track record of those who will take over the mantle of governance from them next year. So I believe that, by the time the next parliament, in which the CPDM will surely be one of the minor opposition parties, is sworn in next year everyone would have realized that an Independent Electoral Commission is an absolute *desideratum* for our democracy.

For this reason, it is very amazing that the French, our most effective neo-colonial masters, gave excuses for not participating in the efforts of other foreign powers to help in the creation of an Independent Electoral Commission and the training of independent election monitors. It is indeed very confusing that, while the French were unwilling to contribute a few hundred thousand CFA francs to this project they have been most willing, with appropriate fanfare and alacrity, to contribute CFA 200 million francs worth of security equipment "to fight crime" in Cameroon. To go by past experience, do we have any guarantee that these sophisticated equipment would not be used in committing rather than fighting crime?

From all indications, the French are still unwilling to align themselves with the democratic forces in this country. We should, however, hold them to their word that it is none of their business whom we choose to elect as our next *"Président de la République,"* come next year. But they should stop deceiving us that the parity of the CFA franc would be maintained after 1999 when the European single-currency, the Euro, comes into effect. How would this be possible when the French are not the ones in control of the *Euro?* Would they be able to help themselves, talk less of helping us ? Did they not continue assuring us that the CFA franc would not be devalued? Should we continue swallowing these things without a pinch of salt?

Written 10/12/96, published Tuesday, January 7, 1996.

17

How to Demystify John Fru Ndi

For quite a long time now I have never written anything directly about John Fro Ndi or Paul Biya, so as not to create or reinforce the erroneous impression that all our problems begin and end with individual personalities. But, as we draw closer to the very decisive 1997 Presidential Elections, which will surely *make or mar* Cameroon, a certain amount of focusing on personalities would be inevitable.

In its secret blueprint (if we are to believe some newspaper reports) to get His Excellency Paul Biya re-elected next year, this time *democratically* (a plausible case of attempted circle-squaring) the ruling CPDM regime has put "demystifying Fru Ndi" high on its agenda. This piece can be considered as a modest contribution to that project; a clear service to the ruling regime for which, as usual, I may receive no thanks. But never mind.

There is no doubt that there is something mythical and almost mystical about John Fru Ndi. It is something very simple but, at the same time, indescribable and unanalyzable. For want of a better word, we can just call it *"Charisma."* It is what creates feverish excitement among the crowds wherever he goes. At Buea last weekend, I beheld, once again, the spectacle of a mother, child gripped under the left arm, racing breathlessly, breasts flapping freely, one slippers lost in the process, to catch just a glimpse of John Fru Ndi, as his convoy was speeding past to the SDF Convention grounds at Mount Mary. It is what makes it completely irrelevant that, before his emergence into the limelight, Fru Ndi was a simple bookseller or whatever; that he doesn't have a doctorate degree, does not communicate *"en français,"* has never been a civil servant and never "treated" administrative "dossiers." It is what makes even genuine intellectuals of the Fonlonian definitional calibre, look somehow puny in his presence, and some rival power-bidders look like bold pretenders. If you know Nelson Mandela very well, then you know what I am struggling to describe. There is something of the Mandela in John Fru Ndi. Go back to *NO TRIFLING MATTER* and refresh your memory with "Under the Magnetic Spell of the Bookseller" (*CAMPOST*, October 23-30, 1992).

Had John Fru Ndi been allowed his victory at the 1992 Presidential Elections, he would, most probably, have already been demystified by now, because actual governing is a great demystifier. This would be particularly so for anybody stepping into the mess and wreckage left by one and a half decades of indescribable rapacious pillage. But, having "stolen" John Fru Ndi's presidential victory, our dictatorship and its foreign neo-colonial manipulators would have done themselves a great favour by leaving him alone. But they went ahead and tried to consolidate their theft, first by imprisoning him in his own house and then attempting to assassinate him in broad daylight. Subsequently, sundry harassment in varying degrees of outrageousness were carried out against him and his party, the Social Democratic Front (SDF), and a total official media blackout imposed on them and their activities. But the man remained undaunted. This is what turned John Fru Ndi from a superman into a divinity. After all, Yondo Black and Albert Mukong who, in terms of chronological time, preceded John Fru Ndi in openly challenging dictatorship in Cameroon are still there with us.

Today, every Cameroonian desirous of change, of salvaging Cameroon from the abyss in which she undeservedly finds herself today, knows that John Fru Ndi is the horse to mount whether you consider him divine or human, charismatic or not, whether you like him or you don't. For sometime now I have observed how, when any other political pretender starts associating with Fru Ndi, his popularity rating among the masses automatically rises. All of Fru Ndi's rivals and co-competitors in the race for the Etoudi Palace know very well that, in a *free and fair* election, none of them, singly or collectively, can make it without Fru Ndi. Let's face facts!

In starting its demystification campaign against Fru Ndi by opening up the official media to him and his activities, the ruling junta is, for once, very well advised. A logical step along this fruitful line would be to organise an American-style live televised debate between John Fru Ndi and his Excellency Professor/Dr. Paul Biya, on why we should vote for each of them next year. I am sure that, as a Doctor and Professor, pitted against a bookseller, the latter would not let down the Americans or the Chinese who awarded him these highly coveted honorific titles, and "the Chairman" would come out of the debate completely disgraced and demystified.

Next, he should be allowed to have his victory in the next elections. The rigours of sheer governance, coupled with his unfamiliarity with administrative "dossiers" will surely complete the demystification of John Fru Ndi and even, probably, reduce him from a divinity to a sub-human. If you doubt this possibility, think back to what you thought of Paul Biya in 1982/83 and compare that to what you think of him today.

That is how to demystify John Fru Ndi. But, beyond both mystification and demystification, how does the CPDM expect us to take them seriously when they are seriously proposing and inviting us to join them atop a dead horse for a ride into the 21st Century? Is the answer blowing anywhere?

Written 171 112/96, published Tuesday, December 24, 1996.

18

If You Saw The Shah Escaping...

Do you remember the Shah of Iran who reigned before the rise of Ayatollah? How funny I cannot now even recall his name! The name was something like Reza Pahlavi, but I may be wrong. In his day as the Shah of Iran he was the richest and most powerful monarch on earth. Besides, he had the backing of one of the most powerful nations on earth which shared with him all the profit from the sale of Iranian petroleum, to the detriment of its impoverished masses. If a dictator could reign for ever, he would have reigned forever. But the Iranian masses sustained their opposition to him and the small clique of fanatical supporters with whom he was sharing Iran's considerable wealth. One fine day, he escaped from Iran in a helicopter, to go and end his days in a cold foreign land, and the Ayatollah Khomeini stepped into his shoes as the new Shah of Iran against the backdrop of incredible popular euphoria.

If you saw or have ever heard about the escape of the Shah, you would not despair about any dictator or dictatorship. No dictatorship or dictator can reign for ever. Is the Malawian "President for life," Kamuzu Banda, not enjoying his retirement from the Malawian Presidency today? Has the one and only Emperor of the Central African Empire, His Majesty Jean Bedel Bokassa, not been recently buried in a shallow grave? The Zairian Marshall still has some mileage before him, but is his final destination not already clearly visible on the horizon? In California, last November, I overheard some Americans discussing his considerable wealth and what is likely to happen to it after his imminent death. So why should we in Cameroon, where we have at least a plausible democratic dictatorship, despair?

After the policy speech of the "natural candidate" of the Cameroon Peoples Democratic Movement (CPDM) at its recent second ordinary congress, which saw a relapse into the fidgety pugilism of 1991/92, many people have been despairing saying: "So this man is really determined to continue in power by all means at all costs?" During that speech, His Excellency certainly forgot that he is the president of all Cameroonians, *sans exclusif.* He forgot to, at least, pretend statesmanship. He sounded like a political thug trying to set the pace and tempo of political thuggery. The CRTV, of course, as usual, praised the speech to high heavens. If His Excellency, instead of reading that his cantankerous speech, had simply coughed, the CRTV would have found a way of highly praising the cough. "His Excellency has coughed. What a wonderful cough! His Excellency is full of pleasant surprises. What do you think of this magnificent royal cough, ABC? ABC: It is really a marvellous cough that only His Excellency could have coughed. With this remarkable cough, His Excellency has set the pace and tempo of all future coughing for all time. Allelu!"

The New Year 1997 address was an overdone attempt to make up for the belligerence, punchiness and sheer arrogance of the congress policy speech. It was simply boring, full of meaningless statistics cum pseudo-facts and figures, and even children could still remark that the man doesn't know what to do with his hands while reading a speech. At some point during the congress, while incredible praise was being heaped on the "natural candidate," the latter seemed so ill-at-ease that at one moment he pocketed his hands sitting on the throne and a kid shouted: "Look he is pocketing his hands!"

His Excellency's determination to continue in power is quite understandable and can even be rightly described as "natural." But what is more important is the determination of Cameroonians to get him out of power and to try another hand at the helm with a different team. *To live is to change and to be perfect is to have changed often.* To refuse change and to persist in a *semper idem* mentality is to preclude any possibility of ever improving our collective lot. His Excellency Paul Biya's idea seems to be that, because he brought democracy to Cameroon, he should be rewarded with the special privilege of continuing with dictatorship. But, quite evidently, he will never be credited with bringing democracy to Cameroon until he gracefully and even cheerfully accepts defeat *in fair and free* elections. He has a great opportunity, once again, to do so soon. And I can predict that, if he does so, he would be forgiven and even given many things in appreciation.

Rumours have started flying around that the ruling CPDM is planning to spring a surprise on Cameroonians by having the parliamentary and presidential elections jointly and by preventing those who have not yet obtained the so-called new national identity card from voting. I think that we should ignore such wicked rumours. His Excellency has already given his word that the coming elections will be free, fair and transparent and that the constitutional time-table will be scrupulously respected. Our neo-colonial masters have also given their word as Gaulic gentlemen that they will not interfere in our political affairs and would respect the democratic choice of Cameroonians. So why all these rumours? We all know that anything to the contrary would be an open invitation to civil strife and war. We are all afraid of war. But it is more important to take steps to prevent war than to waste precious time fearing it. Fear of war alone has never prevented any war. One should never be so afraid of war as to prefer being a slave than wisely struggling for freedom.

My disinterested advice in these columns has usually been ignored by both the government and the opposition. But I will not give up. I will continue trying. Here is another piece of advice as to *how the opposition can proceed* in the forthcoming elections: The much-trumpeted alliance of opposition parties against the ruling *CPDM* should be carefully worked out between the *SDF* and *UNDP* parties on the basis of a very limited transitional programme of say, 12 months. The other opposition parties can then ally or align themselves with either of the two main blocks. Parties which did not boycott the January 1996 Municipal Elections but did not win any municipal councils should simply shut-up for now, lie low and do more work at the grassroots for the future. If we continue taking any Tom, Dick and Harry who declares himself an opposition leader seriously, we could be in for too much confusion and nasty surprises. We should *beware* of yesterday's traitors because they are also tomorrow's potential traitors.

The SDF and UNDP should not dissolve into a single party because we should not risk ending up with another one party state. After the transitional period, during which genuine democratic foundations and structures would have been laid, they should amicably separate and canvass for the support of Cameroonians on the basis of their respective party programmes. Every party should stand or fall on its promised programme and its success in implementing it when elected to power. Seeing how some CPDM barons of yesterday have been posturing and angling for positions, within the SDF, loudly claiming to have *always* been with Fru Ndi in spirit if not in body, it is to be hoped that today's ruling party would not be completely deserted tomorrow. That would be a sad comment on the commitment of Cameroonians to principles and truthfulness. A word to the wise is enough! 1997 is here!! HAPPY NEW YEAR!!!

Written 05/01/97, published Tuesday, January 21, 1997.

19

On Behalf of a College Room-mate

I have once remarked in this column that the bond between school class-mates is much stronger than any tribal bond. People are never so ready to bend or even break the rules of any game as when it is on behalf of a class-mate or school mate. Some of the most formidable mafias you are likely ever to come across are *alumni* mafias, composed of former students of a particular educational institution. You would, no doubt, have heard of the "Kaduna mafia," the "Ibandanites" and the "Lions" in Nigeria. You are surely aware of "Sobans," "Bobans," "Shesans," "Opsans," "Sakerittes" etc., and what they are capable of doing, right here in Cameroon.

One sure way of fighting *tribalism* is to encourage the flourishing of Old Boys Associations, Old (or is it Past?) Girls Associations, Former Students Groups etc., provided, of course, that admission into our educational institutions is not tribalised from the onset with the result that the *alumni* associations become composed exclusively or predominantly of people speaking one *contri-talk*. These are sensitive issues with me because I am a de-tribalised anti-tribalist and an ardent apostle of *meritocracy*. Very soon, under a different *alias* from that of this column, you will be able to read all my essays on the subjects of *Democracy and Meritocracy*, published by Galda and Wilch Verlag, Glienicke-Berlin. But that is a different issue.

I was talking about the power of *alumni* associations. But even stronger than *alumni* bonds are the bonds which bind members of a particular class. Among Sobans, for instance, witness the "Pioneers," "Record Class," "Mbo Boys," "Spirits," "Transition Class," "Cunningham Class," "Brothers of the Coast," "Damian Renovatory Class," etc. Here the bond is much stronger than that between siblings from the same womb.

The only bond that is probably even stronger than that between former classmates is the bond between former College room-mates. It is easy to understand. The High School or College period is the most turbulent, reckless, carefree and experimentive in anybody's life. It coincides with the adolescent/early adulthood period, during which, if you don't try any venture, you will never try it again. Now, it so happens that a room-mate is one person who knows all your most intimate secrets, even those your mother doesn't know, from whom you can hide absolutely nothing-from the fact that you snore like a drunkard at night through the fact that you are in the habit of promising marriage to six different girls at the same time, to your occasional epileptic fainting fits. And for each of your room-mate's six fiancées you have to pretend that she is the only coconut in your good friend's locker, instead of frankly and honestly telling her that another one left two days before her arrival, after 7 hilarious and ecstatic days.

It is amazing what otherwise very principled persons can bring themselves to do on behalf of a former room-mate. You can do for you room-mate what you cannot even do for yourself. In fact, quite recently, I found myself doing for my former room-mate at the University of Ife, Nigeria, what I had long given up doing for myself. I condescended to go to the Ministry of Finance here in Yaounde and follow-up the payment of his salary arrears and unpaid allowances. Now, this is something that I had tried for myself throughout 1993/4 and, after wasting precious time, money and energy to no avail, had given up and vowed never, never to set my foot again in that desolate place called "Minfi" or "Finance." But I was unable to resist breaking my solemn vow on behalf of my former University room-mate when he called from Buea asking me to do him the favour of breaking my solemn vow and doing for him what I could not do for myself.

It is only along this explanatory hypothesis or theory (I dare even say "law") that one can understand His Excellency, Honourable Ouattara, Deputy President of the IMF, who came calling the other day to lie shamelessly about Cameroon's situation vis-à-vis the IMF. There is no African or third-world country undergoing the harsh structural adjustment conditionalities of the IMF that can be said to be doing well. They are not meant to do well. The real purpose of IMF SAP's is to sap industrially underdeveloped countries, create investment channels for the surplus capital of the industrialised predatory nations of the world, and turn all third-world countries, producers of industrial raw-materials, into subservient permanent appendages of their erstwhile colonial masters. Yes, quote me!

It is very ironic that the President of the IMF himself should come here and be assuring us that we are doing very well with the IMF, whereas we should have been the ones trying to convince him that we are doing our best and that the IMF should be patient with us. A young lady working with the IMF here in Yaounde told me: "Don't mind Ouattara! He came here to play politics. Cameroon's situation is very grim indeed." Yes, Ouattara was specially invited to come and help the regime in which his University room-mate and wedding bestman was recently appointed Prime Minister and Head of Government. What is a little *white lie* on behalf of a room-mate? Would you refuse a little favour for your room-mate *cum* wedding bestman, who is the only other living person who knows the "top secret" that you went to bed on your bachelor's eve with someone other than the lady for whom you were answering "I do, I do" the next morning before the priest?

Ever since Honourable Musonge's appointment, I have continued wondering what His Excellency Paul Biya's political calculations were, in appointing someone from a numerical minority, who is simply charming in his honesty and simplicity, with neither the will nor ability for crockery, as the head of a pack of veteran crooks.

Was it, perhaps, on behalf of his former College Room-mate, so that the latter could be invited to come and do what he came and (unsuccessfully) tried to do? Your guess is as good as mine.

Written 21/01/97, published Tuesday, February 4, 1997.

20

Mixed Signals of the Emerging Shape of Things

Faithful watchers of our political thermometer would agree that the political temperature has been dropping towards normality in recent times. Among the factors responsible for this trend, the following can be mentioned:

(1) the highly diplomatic contribution of some foreign missions towards democratisation in Cameroon;

(2) the Social Democratic Front (S.D.F.) party congress in Buea during which the leadership of the party changed its usually highly confrontational tone to a more mature and mellowed one reminiscent of a credible shadow government poised and ready to take up the reins of governance;

(3) the U.N.D.P. party congress in Ngaoundere during which the opposition made common cause and the S.D.F. and U.N.D.P. went into an alliance, backed by a public oath by Ni John Fru Ndi and Maigari Bello Bouba never to betray or let down the "Cameroonian masses;

(4) Prime Minister Peter Mafany Musonge's non-confrontational style of doing things which contrasts sharply with his predecessor's hawkish approach characterised by a philofolly of back-scratching and obsession with *l'autorite de l'état;*

(5) the government's belated acceptance to open up the electoral registers to all eligible citizens under credibly fair conditions without the usual hide and seek and sundry *magu-magu.*

If this trend continues, and if embezzled money, SOCAPALM oil and Korean rice don't start flowing *(awuuf get* bone?) as polling day approaches, then we are poised for a real democratic breakthrough. (By the way if anybody sees where they are eating *avwuf* he should not rush to come and call me. I don't believe in *awuuf*. I relieve in sweating for what I get. Foofoo corn is always very sweet after you have sweated very well). Such a break-through would be in everybody's better interest (as I have never tired of repeating) including the hoodlums who have raped and wrecked our country and nearly ruined our lives. This trend offers an opportunity for the New Deal regime of His Excellency Paul Biya to ease itself out of its embarrassing office without any loss of face and without too many severe and serious consequences.

The press or print media, both private and official has also made remarkable improvements in objective reportage and fair comment. I have once awarded a gold medal to *La Nouvelle Expression* for good investigative journalism on the CELLUCAM AFFAIR. It is my pleasure to pass on the gold medal today to our own CAMEROON POST, with a red feather for Charlie Ndichia, for its investigative story on the long-running and systematised fraud at SONARA. Don't we now understand why the New Deal government stubbornly refused to bring the accounts of SONAEA and SNH to the open even under pressure from the IMF and World Bank? Prophets usually go without honour among their own members of the same household. So let me here also pat Julius Afoni on the back for his interviews which have a way of teasing out very remarkable truths and facts from his interviewees.

It should, however be mentioned that in the trend under focus, the electronic media, alias CRTV is still lagging behind. In political news, the CRTV still has only the CPDM, WCPDM and YCPDM on its agenda, as usual. It is surprising that up till now they have not yet *dementied* that Ni John Fru Ndi went to Rome and met the Pope at the Vatican and shook his hand, discussed with him and received his blessing. This might indicate some positive progress on the part of the CRTV, albeit negatively conceived.

I have followed some of the SDF primaries keenly and they are a great contribution to the democratisation process, in spite of the fact that a few camels seem to have successfully sailed through the democratic eye of the needle. What it all shows is that education and awareness at the grassroots about democracy and meritocracy is very essential in the process. Without such education and awareness, demagogy will always have a role to play and ordinary people will unthinkingly cast their precious vote for the fellow who offered them the last *awuuf* bottle of beer without calculating their middle and long-term interests. The S.D.F. N.E.C. has a very delicate job of balancing *"power to the people!* with sheer credibility and suitability as it works towards a final list out of all the democratically elected hopefuls. But there is no doubt that genuine democracy is at work within the S.D.F. Quite significantly, none of those who finally sail through will have any need of organising the people of his village to send a message of congratulations and thanks to His Excellency Ni John Fru Ndi for appointing one of their own to parliament. Ni John Fru Ndi didn't sit down alone or with a handful of personal cronies and draw up a list the way his New Deal counterpart is wont to do.

The parliamentary elections will obviously not take place according to the constitutional stipulations. But we should ignore these constitutional violations without much fuss if they will help more people to register on the electoral lists and the procedural rules of the game to be made fairer and more transparent. This is a time when Pa Andze Tchoungi's aphorism to the effect that "the law was made for Man and not Man for the law" might be really appropriate. Please, make sure that you are registered for the elections. I am tired of repeating that it is very irresponsible for any Cameroonian to treat this issue with levity.

Written 04/02/97, published Tuesday, March 11, 1997.

21

Address to the Youth

I am talking about my own address to the youths, not about that of His Excellency Paul Biya. I am not a senior political analyst at CRTV to start making a mountain out of a mole-hill or a feast out of a non-event. If HE farts, the CRTV senior political analysts would spend an hour in round-table formation praising the fart. And when they exhaust their originality and ingenuity on fartology, they would turn to the *colour* of his suit, the *design* on his tie, the *shape* of his haircut and his general *look* and praise them highly. I would not like to be a senior analyst at CRTV because you are condemned always to seek and proclaim the positive, even where it does not exist. I don't envy them at all. It is not easy to be saddled with the duty of trying to square the circle every time. It is even easier to be a critic and professional fault-finder like yours truly, even though the consequence is unpopularity with everybody. It would be great if we could just have the political analysis without the speech or address itself, which is what I suggest should be done next time. That way we would not have the feeling of someone playing with our intelligence, telling us a completely different thing concerning what we have just a few moments ago been ear and eye witnesses of.

The 1997 Youth Day Presidential Address had at least one objective positive point that doesn't need a CRTV senior political analyst to point out: it was brief, even if not to the point. Not that brevity, as they say, is the soul of wit, but that, when you have nothing to say, you should keep quiet instead of producing much sound and fury signifying nothing. The address lasted only 7 minutes, which is a record in brevity compared to previous addresses. If I were HE's speech writer it would have been even briefer, lasting no more than 3 minutes. I would have written:

"My dear young Compatriots,

In the past 15 years, I have been making speeches to you on this day. Today will not be an exception, although I really no longer know what to tell you. In the past I have made many promises to you, none of which ever came to pass, through no fault of mine. I will not make any more promises this time around because the basket is now empty. It is not easy to govern, especially a complex and variegated country like Cameroon. You may not believe me until one day it becomes your turn to step into the shoes I am now wearing. After 15 years, I am now weary and no longer seeing *the light at the end of the tunnel* which I was wont to see at least once every year. Is my sight failing, or is there really no light at the end of this tunnel? I don't really know. But this I do know that I badly need a rest (don't mind my youthful appearance and good looks!) and that exactly is what I intend to do. I *will* retire to my green beans and pineapple farm before the end of this year. Don't deceive yourselves into thinking that those merchants of you-know-what that you have abandoned me and are running after, and who are impatiently and immodestly waiting to chop my chair, will necessarily perform better. The World Bank and IMF will not let them. Governing no be small thing, although fools don't know this fact. Best wishes, goodbye and God bless Cameroon." Oh Cameroon...

The second objective positive point that needs no CRTV senior analyst to unearth is that the 1997 Youth Day Speech clearly shows that His Excellency sincerely wants peace in Cameroon. What is not clear is if he has abandoned the philofolly so clearly and eloquently expressed at the Yaounde Municipal Town Hall grounds in 1991 to the effect that *if you want peace you must prepare for war.*

My own address:

Fellow citizens and co-wretches of the earth. Don't be proud that you are young because that is not an achievement. Chronological youth is simply an ineradicable aspect of your bio-data. Physiological and mental youth are very relative. That is why some of you come out old from the womb, as it were, whereas some of your parents and grandparents enjoy perpetual youthfulness, thanks to plastic and transplant surgery and their ability to afford them. For decades you have been deceived with illusory false promises and sweet-sounding shibboleths. What is the use of a Youth Day? Why don't they also celebrate an Old Age Day? If they expect you to be proud of the simple fact of being young, should they not equally be proud of the mere fact of being old? I tell you that the Youth Day was invented to cover up part of the history of this our Banana Republic. Quote me and go and ask teachers of Cameroon history. I am addressing you as a young old man myself. I know without being told that most of you listening to me are old young men yourselves. Just imagine if our two generations joined hands together and decided to take our destiny into our own hands. Do you see us failing? Our anthem would be BEER MUNGO, although the Mungo River is not beer and, if it were, how happy Cameroonians would be!

Long live Cameroon! Yours truly.

Written 11/02/97, published Tuesday, February 25, 1997

22

Registering on the Electoral List

I wonder how the exercise of registering for the forthcoming elections is going in other parts of the country; but in Yaounde it has, so far, been an uphill task for ordinary Cameroonians, in spite of the occasional radio encouragement for people to come out and register. In Yaounde, the exercise is only a shouting distance from a big farce. After about three weeks of patient wind-chasing, I finally managed to get all eligible members of the Gobata household registered. Can we be sure until we have got our voting cards and actually seen our names on the voters' list? You know the answer.

I accidentally discovered that, as far back as last year, clandestine registration teams had gone round the "quartier" from house to house doing registration. But they went only to the houses of *bona fide* Egyptians, skipping the houses of all Jews and all those suspected of Jewish inclinations or sympathies. These are the people whose voting cards were already ready and have been distributed. I am really surprised that they skipped me, implying that they number me among the Jews, whereas whenever I pass by the compound of my "chef de Quartier" I always greet everyone warmly and speak and behave with an expansive and confident mood, like a CPDM baron with strong connections "above" who could easily summon the services of gendarmes anytime. But I begin now to understand why sometime ago they were not only confident but arrogant about the coming elections, saying that they would be free, fair and transparent and that their only problem is those who might want to resort to violence after the results are announced. If the elections are free, fair and transparent, why would anybody contest the results, talk less of resorting to violence? The answer is blowing in the wind.

Every Cameroonian has a serious patriotic duty to spare no efforts in ensuring that all eligible voters, beginning with and including himself/herself, are registered for voting in the forthcoming elections. Voting itself is a sacred duty for which no excuses are permissible. Apathy in this situation is criminal and almost tantamount to treason, because what we are risking, if the forthcoming elections are not overwhelmingly clear, is a situation that could easily catapult us into a Rwanda, a Burundi or a Zaire. Power is delightful and absolute power is absolutely delightful. For this reason, people who wield dictatorial power will always need very definite and determined "encouragement" from those under their rule to quit the stage. Who would have believed that, up to the present moment, the Field Marshall of Zaire would still be hanging on both to life and power?

In Cameroon, we have a really golden opportunity to pull things off peacefully and democratically. We must not allow our determination to waver or our efforts to slacken. In this regard, it is to be hoped that Ni John Fru Ndi and Bello Bouba Maigari would keep their pledge not to betray the Cameroonian masses. The forthcoming elections will be fought between the SDF-UNDP alliance and the CPDM and its allies and satellites. There will be no middle ground and everyone had better position themselves in either of the two camps so that we could have a real match instead of causing confusion all over the place.

For unfathomable reasons, *Le Messager*, which we have always credited with the honorific title of "*doyen*" of fearlessly objective journalism, mischievously and maliciously put false words into John Fru Ndi's mouth, which nowhere appeared in their purported interview, to the effect that he (John Fru Ndi) does not "discuss with small leaders." This would have been quite false since, until quite recently, he spent most of his time discussing with small leaders. But, even though Fru Ndi never made the statement falsely credited to him, he ought to have made it, in the light of past experience.

There is nothing like "the opposition" in the abstract. We should be talking about political parties and their militants and programmes, the fact notwithstanding that there are people, like yours truly, who belong to no political party but who are all for change and the instauration of genuine democracy and who could never cast their vote for the incumbent dictatorship.

Whenever there is talk of "the opposition" in vague abstract terms, then people like Gustav Essaka, Louis Tobie Mbida, Jean Jacques Ekindi and their likes, who own militantless parties but are eloquent and loquacious, start mounting the rostrum with characteristic orchestrated cacophonic noises, hoping to ride rough-shod into power on the back of some donkey. Are these the "leaders" John Fru Ndi should be sitting down to discuss with everyday? These "small" (an accurate descriptive term) leaders would do well, in their own interest, and that of us all, to join any of the credible formations without any further delay, instead of making confusion their stock-in-trade.

Well, I know that "the Spirit" has not been coining your way with the desired regularity. No fault of Gobata's. *Cameroon Post* (New Look) seems to be still beset with many procedural problems. If a piece sent to the HQ in Buea from Yaounde through the recommended channels of the hierarchy itself has not reached its destination after two weeks, then can all be well? As a consequence, you have often been served a slightly stale menu. The *Spirit* could be making an emergency landing soon, but, in any case, not before singing *NUNC DIMITTIS* with Simeon.

Written 25/02/97, published Tuesday, March 11. 1997.

23

In Provisional Praise of Paul Biya

I could easily become a frequent praise-singer of His Excellency Paul Biya, if the latter continues changing and improving at the remarkable rate that he has displayed in recent times. "To live is to change and to be perfect is to have changed often." You have heard this from me several times before. I am first and foremost a critic (a thankless profession) to the point of being critical even about my own criticism. So don't be surprised if I start sounding like those CRTV fellows I have often criticised, if only HE continues and improves on the present trend. I give praise where it is due and blame where it is due.

It might have escaped the notice of most Cameroonians, but His Excellency Paul Biya has recently departed remarkably from his normal practice in a positive direction. Such remarkable positive departure could not miss my critical attention. First of all, on so-called Youth Day, HE abandoned his French suits and came out in ordinary shirt and trousers, Mandela-style, and shook hands with excited children like the ordinary mortal that he is. We could soon see him, one fine day, in an African dress.

Secondly, for several months running now, His Excellency has not gone on any "short private visit" abroad. Moreover, he has recently, for the first time in history, spent nearly a whole week in a town in Cameroon (Kribi) other than Yaounde or Mvomeka'a. Is it not possible that he might have discovered the advantages of Kribi over Switzerland and Baden Baden?

How lucky Kribi is! In terms of the back-scratching philofolly of the New Deal regime, Kribi has no rival. If the people of Kribi were to reciprocate accordingly, they would scratch Biya's back until it starts peeling off. What I don't understand are reports that the **S.D.F.** and other opposition parties have made significant inroads in the Kribi area. Is back-scratching working at all? Your opinion would be as good as mine. But just consider the facts. Kribi got the deep sea port and oil pipe-line from Chad (both in preference to

Victoria alias Limbe which was highly favoured by neutral economic experts). Now Kribi has got its own oil field inaugurated and there is increasing talk of its becoming the industrial base of this our rough triangle.

Of course, Kribi, just like any other part of this country, has every legitimate right to these facilities. Were it not for the "**autochthones-allogenes**" companion philofolly to these things, would many of us not start rushing down to Kribi now to see whether we could make a living there? When some years ago I timidly suggested that his Excellency seemed bent on transferring the economic and industrial base of the country to the Centre-South, I was nearly painted in the gaudy colours of an enemy of the New Deal. But I had heard high rumours about the possibility of a Fang Republic.

If HE's praise-worthy positive trend continues, he should also be spending a week in Buea or Victoria or Likomba in the not-to-distant future. He could tie a wrapper (with red stockings and a broom?) while *the* Madam wears a *kaba* and they could play with children at the Victoria beach or Botanical Gardens. But what would he tell the people of the South West Province? If he has not abandoned the back-scratching mentally before then, the only thing, surely, that he can say is that he scratched their back with a Prime Minister and Head of Government. Should they not ask him why he didn't scratch their back instead with the deep sea port and oil pipe-line and give the P.M. to Kribi? After all, Massa Yo who is from Kribi is not only very-good Prime Ministerial material but used to be, until quite recently, the de *facto* Prime Minister of the Republic.

The only thing about the praise-worthy one week stay in Kribi is that it occurred at a time that His Excellency should have been in Gaborone, Botswana, for the meeting of the Commonwealth leaders. There, he would have had the rare opportunity of coming face to face with John Fru Ndi, for the first time since the latter's May 26, 1990 earth-shaking revolution, and shaking hands (warmly or coldly) with him. This would really have demonstrated to the whole world that our democracy is on the good foot. Do we really have to wait for October 1997 to witness this long-awaited handshake during a putative change of guard and handing-over ceremony? Only time will tell. But did HE go to Kribi to escape going to Gaborone? Your guess should be as good as mine.

But it is very worrying that, in spite of workshops and seminars to teach journalists and media people objectivity and fair play, as and aid to democratisation, the CRTV people have refused to learn anything. Last Sunday *"Cameroon Calling"* (admittedly a poor caricature of its former self) presented only the ruling CPDM's side of the Gaborone story and boldly lied that both Bello Bouba Maigari and John Fru Ndi were still out of the country. In actual fact, John Fru Ndi had been back into the country since the previous Friday and no attempt whatsoever was made to get in touch with him. I confirmed this personally from him. I have said it before that, to accurately monitor the democratisation process in Cameroon, one only needs to observe the CRTV. I still stand by that claim.

Written 05/03/97, published Tuesday, March II, 1997.

24

Constitutional Council: Why we Are Worried

The last (extraordinary) session of our now expired parliament was evidently not convened to create the (as yet) non-existent Constitutional Council. The Constitutional Council was already created by the new constitution on 18th January 1996. The functions of the Constitutional Council as promulgated envisaged in the above constitution are to ensure the regularity of elections as well as to proclaim the results. Left as it is in the January 1996 constitution, one could more easily believe Pa Andze Tsoungi's claim that it is a cautious way of gradually working towards an independent electoral commission. The last very brief extraordinary session of parliament was evidently summoned to make the Constitutional Council the sole and only body to proclaim election results and to make such proclamation unchallengeable in any court of law or other putative jurisdiction. These specifications evidently have turned the as yet non-existent Constitutional Council into a putatively anti-democratic instrument that could possibly turn out to be the greatest retrogressive set-back to our struggling democracy. It is really amazing that our so-called people's representatives could unthinkingly approve such amendments of the electoral law.

What the recent amendments have done is to effectively put the Constitutional Council above the law. My first worry then is the same as that which led me to suggest to Honourable Bouba Bello Maigari that the title of the Private Members Bill that he and the U.N.D.P. party wanted to pass through parliament should be "Independent Electoral Commission" and not "Autonomous Electoral Commission" because it is undesirable to create any commission that would be a law-giver unto itself. How does the announcement of election results by the Divisional Supervisory Committees prevent the Constitutional Council from announcing and proclaiming the final overall results? Would such a procedure not be indisputably more transparent in that any objective neutral observer who cared to follow the Divisional results could simply compute them to confirm the veracity and validity of the pronouncements of the Constitutional Council unchallengeable in Law? Is that not to imbue the Constitutional Council with divine attributes and prerogatives? The answer to all these questions is blowing in the wind.

We might have been less sceptical if the said Constitutional Council had already been created and if we knew that each and every one of its members was a Cameroonian of unquestionable integrity who can neither be bribed nor bullied. Do we have any good reason to believe that when the Constitutional Council comes to be created it would be composed of Cameroonians of such calibre? In fact, how many proven Cameroonians of such a descriptive calibre do we know to exist? To make things worse, the recent amendments have been spear-headed by none other than Honourable Pa Andze Tsoungi and Honourable Professor Augustine Kontchou Koumegni. We have not forgotten 1992 and the highly controversial Presidential Elections of that year nor the role played by the above duo in the eventual maintenance of the status quo.

So how can we be assured? What reason do we have for supposing that they have not already cooked up in advance the results that the Constitutional Council would proclaim when it comes into being. Furthermore, it is worrying that the amendments ostensibly meant to make the elections more transparent have been accompanied by emphasis on and obsession with maintaining peace and order and containing any violence. One thing that is absolutely certain is that if the elections are free and fair and transparent, there would be no violence. If the will of the majority of Cameroonians is allowed to prevail in the forthcoming elections, then we are surely headed for peace and tranquillity and prosperity as we have never known before. If not, we are as surely headed in the opposite direction. Let us learn in good time the lessons that we ought to learn from South Africa, on the one hand, and Rwanda, Burundi and Zaire, on the other hand. Don't get me wrong. I am a critic and sceptic, but not a pessimist. I have not said that the Constitutional Council will fail us. We cannot say that for sure in advance. But our premonitions are reasonable and justified.

We are no strangers to democratic rhetoric and bold pretences accompanied by the most unbelievably flagrant anti-democratic practices. You have read the speech of the British High Commissioner, Nicholas McCarthy, delivered on the occasion of a human rights seminar in Garoua on 24th February 1997. How can we reconcile the fact that a government which has been talking so much about democracy and free, fair and transparent elections should be so much against gratuitous initiatives by those who really know that democracy is all about to organise human rights seminars, train municipal mayors in democratic practices or independent electoral monitors and observers? The answers to all these questions I am raising are blowing in the wind.

As for the challengeability of the proclamations of the yet to be created Constitutional Council, we need to be reminded that what cannot be challenged in court can be challenged outside the court and ought to be challenged if it is really challengeable.

Written 17/03/97, published Tuesday, March 25, 1997

25

For Every Mobutu a Kabila

When His Excellency, Marshall Sese Seko Mobutu was recently persuaded to interrupt his terminal cancer treatment in France and return to Zaire because his empire was collapsing at an alarming rate, he reached Zaire and refused to show his face, thereby giving cause for wild speculations. Those who had gone to the airport to receive Mobutu. including journalists and even the little flower girls were chased away without any explanation. Some people thus started speculating that, maybe, the presidential plane had come empty or even that he may have passed out on the way. But two days later, the Leviathan emerged and announced, *"Je m'appelle Mobutu"* (My name is Mobutu). Apparently, he needed to assure everyone that they were not seeing a ghost. *Me voici à Douala* type of thing, *quoi*. Maybe he equally needed to reassure himself. He is hanging on precariously to both life and power, as prostate cancer and Laurent Kabila close in on him decisively.

What account can Mobutu give of himself and his over three decades of absolute rule in this his final hour of both power and life, before Zairians, humanity and God? He came into power under the guise of a Messiah and took control of one of the richest African countries. He is now bowing out of life and power as one of the richest individuals in the world while Zaire has assumed the status of one of the poorest countries on earth.

Mobutu declared that he hadn't returned to Zaire to take care of his so-called financial empire which everyone likes talking about but rather in the interest of unity and peace in his country. If he really wants unity, peace and well-being in his country, do you think he doesn't know what to do? If he were patriotic and wanted to do Zaire and Zairians a parting favour, would he not have thrown in the towel, even this belatedly, and left them to sort out themselves and their lot as best as they can? What can Mobutu now do for Zaire? After over three decades of indescribable rape and pillage and plunder, (are you familiar with that description?) what can he again salvage? Is it possible to crush a tender flower or rape an innocent child and then undo the act again?

The OAU conference recently held in Lome, Togo, to "prevent disaster in the *Grands Lacs* region," has all the outline elements of farcical play-acting. What are we supposed to make of the likes of the Eyademe of Togo, Abacha of Nigeria and ours truly of Cameroon sitting down and piously and solemnly calling for peace, dialogue and reconciliation in Zaire? These are the Does of Africa whose litany we sang long ago. Each of them has his own Kabila. Why don't they each reconcile with their own respective Kabilas, ensure dialogue, peace and reconciliation in their own respective kingdoms before trying to remove the speck in their neighbour's eye? Was their pretentious meeting not, perhaps, called in solidarity with their chum, Mobutu, to slow down Kabila or prevent him from completing his messianic mission?

If Kabila really understands his messianic mission, he should march on without paying any attention to the empty noises coming from Lome to subvert his salvific mission. But once his mission is accomplished, he should retire and withdraw from the scene. This is the aspect of messianism that every messiah, so far, except Jesus their/prototype, has failed to comprehend. No messiah can really govern, except from a safe distance like heaven, without the risk of ending up as a Doe. The Kingdom of every true messiah is *not of this world* where power tends to corrupt and absolute power corrupts absolutely. My honest advice to Laurent Kabila would be that he should complete the liberation of Zaire, supervise free, fair and transparent democratic elections, and then retire from both the army and public life.

The path to political immortality lies in not clinging on to power. If our own Mobutu were to throw in the towel, even this belatedly, he would, at least partially, be politically immortalised. Many people don't realise that the main reason we are often nostalgic about Ahidjo, in spite of his dictatorship, is that he voluntarily (whether willingly or unwillingly) gave up power. Had Ahidjo continued clinging on to the absolute power he was wielding until his death, he would surely have ended up in the rubbish dump of our history. As it is, he does have a place which will surely become clearer once the present dispensation yields place (whether willingly or otherwise) to a new. Whether his hand-picked successor will equally find a place beside him depends on his ability to refrain from clinging on to power. Go and ask Hons. Mboui and Nsahiai.

The Americans who helped in making Mobutu what he is, and who would now happily help in unmaking him, say that they have no apologies, that they don't have to be living in the past. We can learn something from here. We don't have to be living in the past. We don't have to be clinging to obsolete structures, systems, ideologies, regimes and personalities when better new alternatives arc available. Hello. French Masters!, are you also learning, as your empire continues collapsing all over Africa?

Written 30/03/97, published Tuesday, April 8, 1997.

26

Killing an Innocent Person Can Never Be Justified

K illing an innocent person is unjustifiable, not only from the point of view of morality but from the point of view of mere rationality. To shed innocent blood is both morally reprehensible and irrational. It is even doubtful whether it is morally right and rational to shed uninnocent blood. In other words, it is doubtful whether it is right or even rational to kill, say, certain criminals. That is why the campaign against *capital punishment* has gained currency in many parts of the world today. This campaign would have been completely victorious were it not that it is very hard to defend the right to life of certain criminals such as those, precisely, who shed innocent blood with levity.

It is also morally reprehensible and irrational to inflict unnecessary pain on any sentient creature. Only pure *sadism* can be responsible for the infliction of such needless pain on any creature with the capacity to suffer, complimented by the capacity to experience pleasure and joy. That is why torture is morally wrong and irrational and the United Nations and Human Rights Organisations the world over have tried to abolish it all over the world.

I don't want to start re-reading for you the final chapters of *The Past Tense of Shit (Book One)* nor do I want to believe that we are about to start re-living the year 1992 which I believed and still hope is already firmly buried in our shitty past. But the recent acts of terrorism in the North West Province should give all of us cause for grave concern. Violence can never solve any human problems; it creates and complicates them. If violence could solve human problems, it would long have solved the problem between the Palestinians and the Israelis in the Middle East. But there is no doubt that after all the violence and innocent killings, after all the waste, the problems of the Middle East, the problems of "God's own chosen people" would be solved, if at all, by simple reconciliatory dialogue, by a simple return to rationality. If violence could solve any human problems, it would surely have solved the problems of Algeria which, since the 1950's, has claimed thousands of innocent lives. But, as I am writing this, there is news about the brutal massacre again of over 80 people, mostly women and children, in Algeria. What problem can be solved by beheading an innocent child with a chain saw? If violence could solve any problems, Nelson Mandela and P. W. de Klerk would not have needed reconciliatory dialogue to achieve what they have achieved for South Africa.

The causes of irrational immorality which manifests itself through violence, the shedding of innocent blood and the infliction of needless pain are not far to seek. They are, variously, blatant injustice, arrogant oppression and suppression, the will to power and domination. The will to power and domination of Adolf Hitler and the small circle of his German supporters led directly to the Second World War whose effects have made the modern world what it is. Some of such effects are the *"might is right"* syndrome and the consequent emphasis on production and proliferation of deadly weapons. Blatant injustice and arrogant oppression and suppression always elicit violence, even self-destructive violence, as the only possible response. Any situation that can push anybody into a suicidal response as the only way of making a point should make us all to stop and think again.

A public and speedy unmasking of the terrorists who operated in the North West Province recently is really desirable. It is equally desirable that the incidents should not be used as an excuse to traumatise ordinary and evidently innocent citizens. A man comes out of his house to urinate in his cassava farm and is arrested and taken into detention. Someone going from one village to sell cocoyams in another is arrested and taken into detention as a suspect because s/he does not have his/her identity card or has only an expired one. A market crowd is herded like cattle and left standing like corn in the rain for hours for a crime they have not even heard about. These things traumatise a community.

Only two official allegations have been adduced, so far, to explain the recent terrorism in the North West Province. The first was that it was the work of bandits. This is an unlikely hypothesis, given both the scale and *modus operandi* of the terroristic acts. The second is that it is the work of Southern Cameroons separatists. As an active participant in AACI (1993) and AACII (1994) and AACIII if and when it is convened: as someone who, since 1990, has tried to give conceptual clarity to the so-called *Anglophone problem*: as one of those who contributed in coining and popularising the slogan **"force of argument and not argument of force,"** I am very-sceptical about this allegation. Not that the Southern Cameroons cause lacks extremists, but that such extremists have been an insignificant minority all along, as can be seen from the *Buea Declaration* and the *Bamenda Proclamation*. Why would the SCNC want to resort to terrorism on the eve of a democratic breakthrough in Cameroon, after which its long-ignored **force of argument** and politico-legal case pending before the United Nations are bound to receive due and deserved attention? The answer is really blowing in the wind. Anybody pretending to be fighting for the cause of Southern Cameroons who could think of carrying out such dastardly acts at such a time must be a really big yamhead. I am very sceptical about this second hypothesis. It does not stand to reason. If a third hypothesis is not discovered or invented or advanced, this one really needs to be proved beyond all doubt. Otherwise, it does not even sound plausible. Let this not be swept under the carpet again as usual. Let us try to get to the bottom of this, this time around.

Written 07/04/97, published Friday April 26, 1997.

27

On the Threshold of a Democratic Breakthrough

Today, in Cameroon, we are standing on the threshold of a democratic breakthrough from the strangulating grip of the repressive dictatorship under which we have been groaning since 1966, and the rapacious plunder that we have all witnessed since the mid-1980s. You may be quite surprised at my optimism, given the very recent indications that our own brand of dictatorship (or advanced democracy, if you prefer) has no intention of simply throwing in the towel and that there is no end to the devious methods and means of survival at its disposal. But, believe me, yours truly, on the basis of my past record. I am often far-sighted (not an ophthalmological ailment) because I am always gazing ahead even when something right on the table (or is it on the ground?) is distracting all of us. Who believed me when I predicted the imminent collapse of Apartheid in South Africa and the victorious triumph of Nelson Mandela? Who took me seriously when, not so long ago, I started talking confidently about the collapse of the French empire in Africa or of the end of Marshall Mobutu?

As a critic cum sceptic but not a pessimist, I usually sight the silver linings beyond several horizons of dark clouds from a respectable distance. Cameroon is on the threshold of a democratic breakthrough and the New Deal regime of His Excellency Paul Biya is about to fall a great fall, after hanging on precariously, for several years, from the rafters of illegitimate dictatorial power. I had wondered on this same page how the new dealers expected us to take them seriously when they were proposing to transport us on top of a dead horse into the 21st century, but no one cared to answer me.

But Ayissi Mvodo had come out with the first broom and started clearing the accumulated cobwebs of delusive illusions. Then we heard incredible diatribe against HE and the New Deal from erstwhile staunch supporters like Ngijol Ngijol Pierre, who terrorised both staff and students on behalf of the New Deal in the heady early 90's, as *Monsieur le Doyen* of the Faculty of Arts, Letters and Social Sciences of Yaounde University; from Albert Ndzogang, who all along had been secretly nursing legitimate ambitions to replace his Master; or from Douala Moutoume, who in 1992 foamed at the mouth in defence of the stolen victory. I have been worried that today's ruling party, even though surely headed for a landslide failure in the coming elections, may not be completely empty of members tomorrow. There are at least some people one would expect to swim or sink with Biya to the end, come what may. But, from the look of things, would Paul be left only with his *allogènes anglo* Peters, Johns and Ephraims? It would be very sad, and. indeed a sad comment on the moral inglorious moment. Beer is left standing alone the rain.

That is why I had very mixed feelings when, on Saturday 12th April 1997, I learned that Pa Foch had uncharacteristically deserted the camp and "gone ahead." Everyone was asking: "How did he die?" when they heard the news and showing disappointment to learn that he died a perfectly natural death, as if God is a human being who pays people in their own coins. As the hangman of two successive dictators, whom he served with unquestionable fidelity, and as the terror of all Cameroonians bold enough to harbour any "subversive" thoughts, it is admittedly hard to believe that Pa Foch could just decide to pass away so easily, without even a token fight, as if he were some ordinary mortal. Was it *les moyem* or *la volonté* of which he used to assure us with a real bully's wide open eyes most convincingly, that was lacking? He who stood so firmly and shamelessly partisanly behind the New Deal, ready to take off his policeman's uniform at any time to dance CPDM *mbaya,* how could he desert the camp at such a critical moment? The answer, my dear friend, is blowing in the wind, the answer is blowing in the wind! We will propose no epitaph for the spot where he is buried. In Book Two of the Past Tense... we had already done (in advance) what ought to be done on the spot. Oh yes, they shat we spat.

And here again comes Titus Edzoa. Would Caesar not surely exclaim: *Et tu Brute!* before giving up the ghost? Who would be next? Your guess is as good as mine. But one thing I cannot understand, maybe you do. Why does everyone who deserts Biya want to be a presidential candidate? Is it a virus infection or something? In any case, let some of these presidential candidates know that some Cameroonians, rightly or wrongly, believe them to have committed or commissioned murder or man slaughterers, they should first clear their good names and clean their soiled reputations convincingly, before asking us to use our votes to escort them to Unity Palace.

We are on the threshold of a democratic breakthrough although we must be very careful about the last desperate kicks of any dying horse.

Written 25/04/1997, published Monday, May 5, 1997.

28

Yielding Place to a New Order

No human being is immortal. No human being is eternal. No human being is omniscient. No human being is omnipotent. No human being is infallible. All human beings are, by their very nature, weak, mortal, transient and fallible. That being the case, no human system or organisation can last for ever. And even if any could last for ever, it ought not.

"The old order changeth, yielding place to new, and God fulfils himself in many ways." Let's not worry- about who said this or even whether s/ he has been accurately quoted. Every human society must create room and make ample allowance in its collective psyche for the old order to change and yield place to a new one. Any society which does not make room for change and renewal denies God, as it were, the opportunity to fulfil his plans, the possibility to work marvels for that society.

"So that one good system may not spoil the world." A system, no matter how good, would cause great damage if it were to be adopted and maintained as the sole, permanent and unchanging system. Just think of what would happen to the world if young human or even animals were not constantly born and grow up to take over from old ones: if crops did not mature to be harvested and fresh ones planted. That would signal the death of the entire world, as we know it. Ditto for any human system, no matter how perfect it may pretend to be. To live is to change and to even approach or approximate perfection is to have changed often. Too much of, even a good thing, is a bad thing.

You may think that I am just rambling speculatively. But just take the example of, say, the United Kingdom of Great Britain. Last week the people of the U.K. overwhelmingly elected the Labour Party of Tony Blair to take over from the Tories of John Major (or should it be Minor?) and to oversee their collective affairs and guide their destiny for the next five years. How do you explain the great excitement of Britons over a new regime, given that the old one was not at all bad and, in any case, nothing close to the sort of disaster that we have here? That is because a new government gives the whole system a new lease of life, a veritable breath of fresh air, even though it is not likely to be infallible. The conservatives and their Thatcher legacy must have done something right and good for the U.K. But when a regime, even a good one, stays on in power for too long, good governance is no longer its objective but rather continuous maintenance of power. That is how corruption and fowl play become its *modus operandi*. As far back as 1993, while on a visit to the U.K., I had noticed that the Conservative regime had lost grassroots support all over the U.K. It should have thrown in the towel then but continued on in power through stratagems and the art of make-believe. Here in Cameroon, the New Deal regime.

With its Ahidjo legacy lost all popular support about a decade ago and should have thrown in the towel then, but has continued on in power through stratagems, empty rhetoric, the art of make-believe, skilful use of violence and repression, etc.

Cameroonians owe themselves the duty, in the interest of collective survival, to escort the CNU/CPDM New Deal regime out of power with alacrity, in spite of whatever putative good it might have done in the past. We should give ourselves a breath of fresh air and a new lease of life and usher in a new regime and a new order, in spite of whatever mistakes it might make in the future. But who will retain our right to criticise, to praise and applaud, to blame and condemn and, above all, to **vote out** any future government and regime that has outlived its usefulness or that we no longer perceive as capable of satisfying our collective interests. That is what I understand by *democracy*: a system that permits peaceful change of the guards and guardians of our collective interests and well-being, a smooth yielding of the old order to a new-one.

Talking about voting, I must place it on record here that I have not yet got my voter's card since registering in January. And the elections are only ten day away, as I am writing this and they keep giving me empty assurances that the cards will come before polling day. Do I have to go and be sleeping in the court-yard of the *chef de quartier* in order to be able to discharge my civic duty? The authorities have announced a drastic drop in the total number of voters by comparison with 1992, without advancing any reasons for such a drop. Is our population decreasing instead of increasing? Are the reasons for the drop not very apparent? Whatever the case, I don't believe that there can be up to one hundred (a generous estimate) Cameroonians who, before God, man and their own consciences, would in the secrecy of a voting booth, cast a vote for the old order to continue. Rational serf-interest does not permit it. So, God bless you as you cast your vote to sack the old pack of crooks and usher in a fresh new order and dispensation.

Written 07/05/1997, published Monday, May 12, 1997.

29

Mola Njoh Litumbe's Concept of Home

According to Mola Njoh Litumbe, a person's home is where that person (or, more accurately, his/her corpse) is going to be taken for burial. This very interesting stipulative definition has the consequence, *inter alia*, that no one knows his/her home, since no one knows where s/he (or, more properly, his/her corpse) is going to be taken for burial. No human being can know, in advance, when or where s/he will die, much less where or how his/her corpse will be buried. S/he can only know these facts post-humously, on condition that post-humous existence is possible as most of us believe it is.

Mola Litumbe does not, however, see or, in any case, he does not draw these logical consequences of his own stipulative definition of home. If we adopt his definition, we would have to wait till after death to know anybody's home, by which time it is too late for Mola to put his strange definition into the use for which it was intended. Honourable Litumbe is working within the philofolie of *autochtones* and *allogènes* elaborated by the New Deal regime in its terminal stage and the consequences he draws from his stipulative definition of home are the following:

(1) "Settlers" in the South West Province are settlers even if they were born there and not Southwesterners because, when they die, they are invariably carried to be buried elsewhere.

(2) It is therefore right to require them to produce a residence permit before being registered for any elections in Cameroon.

(3) As a mark of gratitude for the hospitality of their indigenous "landlords," settlers in Bakweriland should support and obey Peter Mafany Musonge (by voting for Paul Biya and the CPDM) so that he can reign as Prime Minister and Head of Government for as long as possible.

It is hard to believe that Mola Njoh Litumbe is not only a member but the leader of an opposition party, albeit a militantless one. When the LDA party was formed, I had the impression, from its declarations and emphases, that it was either trying to usurp the place of or to duplicate SWELA. There was so much emphasis on the South West that it could appropriately be called the political wing of the South West Elites Association, and I told Simon Munzu, one of its founding fathers, so at the time. A political party ought to have a more national outlook even if it originates from and/or is based in a particular locality. As things have turned out, the LDA has not been able to hold itself together in the South West because the impulse of parochialism has its limits only in egoistic individualism.

Mola Njoh Litumbe's party or whatever remains of it would do better to dissolve itself into SWELA because of its very parochial and inward-looking attitude. There is, of course, nothing wrong with pressure groups or development associations such as SWELA, NOCUDA, LAAKAM, etc. But such should never be confused with political parties because their commitment is localised or particularised, whereas a political party, in our context, must, at least, have national vision and aims, if not spread. One of the things which confirmed for me that the recent terrorism in the North West Province was a mounted scam is that, when I read the analysis of French papers and magazines such as *Jeune Afrique* and *Jeune Afrique Economie*, which all claimed to have done "exhaustive investigations" on the ground, they were constantly referring to the SCNC as a political party which, in spite of its secessionist agenda, was allowed to operate because of the democratic magnanimity of the Biya regime. How could the SCNC be a political party when it includes members of nearly all major political parties? Today there are supposed to be about 150 registered political parties in Cameroon. Over 90% of them cannot pass my definition of a political party.

Power and desperation, the will to power and, particularly, the will to desperately maintain already acquired power can lead even very good people to do a lot of evil and harm. There are some high-flight members of the New Deal Presidential Majority with whom I used to associate very closely (as intellectuals and all that) before their elevation to the high table of real political and economic power.

Ever since, I can simply not believe the sort of things they can bring themselves to do on behalf of the New Deal nor the utter rubbish that they are capable of boldly pronouncing before a microphone or television camera.

His Excellency, President Paul Biya, has never and cannot go out to campaign in spite of his desperate need to stay in power because, if he stands on a campaign dais before a mixed crowd of Cameroonians, he cannot have anything coherent, much less convincing, to say, especially in Southern Cameroons. He needs his Peters and Ephraims and Johns to shine his shit for him. By the time Honourable Peter Mafany Musonge is through with campaigning for Paul Biya, he will no longer be recognizable as the once remarkable technocrat that we all knew and admired before his elevation to the power of being close to power (*Corruptio optima pessima!*). The degeneration of a good person or thing is so much to be regretted.

Note that the SDF campaign team recently stoned out of Musonge's village (with at least his tacit, if not explicit approval) was not composed of *allogènes* arrogantly and ungratefully preying on Bakwerians, but of full-blooded *bona fide* Bakwerians. Are these anti-democratic fanatics at the peripheries aware that, at the centre itself, things have completely *fallen apart* and that *the centre no longer holds*? Against Njoh Litumbe's definition of home, I am proposing the following for the careful attention of our new parliament as they settle down to the initial task of providing us with a democratic Constitution: *Home for any Cameroonian is anywhere s/he chooses to make it.*

Written 14/05/1997, published Wednesday, May 21, 1997.

30

As a Participant Observer

As a participant observer, it is *my* patriotic duty to make the following report on our just-ended parliamentary elections. I do know that some non-participant international observers came to witness these elections and it would be very interesting to know their impressions and to read their own report. But there are aspects of our attempts at democratisation that someone who has not closely followed our story since 1990, would not be able to appreciate. Since 1990, the ruling regime in Cameroon has tried to be very democratic in its language and declarations and in everything that has to do with form and appearances; but it has determinedly moved in the opposite direction regarding everything that has to do with substance and the actual reality on the ground. The truth is that the ruling regime in Cameroon, which has remained as dictatorial as any overt and unpretentious dictatorship, has progressively rendered the rules of the political game vaguer and more fluid so as to manipulate them at will and thus continue staying on in power. No real democratic structures have been laid and the modicum that was there before has been progressively destroyed. After undergoing a thousand and one arbitrary tinkerings, the Constitution, the supreme law of the land, is less democratic, less just and less fair than the overtly monolithic constitution from which it has evolved. This is a remarkable fact.

How can we explain the fact that the President of the Republic is still capable of changing the electoral law by a simple presidential decree signed at midnight, for an election that has already taken place and managing to give it retroactive effect, as he did a few days ago? This is a really scandalous action that shows an unbelievable determination to manipulate things and bend the rules so as to continue hanging on to power. How do we explain the fact that today (1997) there are fewer people registered on the electoral lists than in 1992 and that many of those registered have not been able to vote either because their voting cards were nowhere to be found or their names were not in any of the registers at the indicated polling booth? By the way, I did manage both to get my voter's card and to actually cast my vote. But it is very significant that this was the very first time I have succeeded in exercising my franchise. Like Nelson Mandela, I have waited for decades to be able to cast a vote, but, unlike Mandela, I did not cast it in an election that can be described as free and fair. Many of my contemporaries and fellow so-called intellectuals were unable to exercise their franchise, in spite of their efforts to do so. This is a very unusual state of affairs. Here in Yaounde, a few days to the elections, potential electors were chased with machetes by thugs of the ruling regime, acting under the cover of members of the armed forces, when they turned out in great numbers to collect their voters' cards following a pretentious radio announcement by the authorities. As it turned out, all these cards had, probably, been made but were withheld so as to be used in the process of frauding. In every polling station, heaps of uncollected voter's cards, belonging to unknown persons, were on display (for the attention of foreign observers?) whereas crowds of potential voters who registered in the said stations could not find their cards. Is this coincidental to allegations that many militants of the ruling party were able to vote several times? And what about the clandestine voting points one, at least, of which was discovered in my "quartier"?

Now, looking back, why did the ruling regime refuse with such determination, against tremendous popular pressure, the idea of an independent electoral commission? What necessitated the specification that the election results would only be announced by a body in Yaounde whose decisions could not be challenged in court or anywhere else? Why did the idea of training Cameroonian independent election observers and monitors, funded by some western countries, so upset the regime and its Godfathers that they proscribed it? In spite of the law about the proclamation of election results, the CRTV, since the night of the elections, has been announcing results according to what they call certain *"tendences"* by which the ruling party has already won an absolute majority in parliament! Is that a way of preparing all of us for accepting the unacceptable? For any one who followed the campaigns for these elections all over the national territory and who is in touch with the masses at the grassroots, the CPDM winning the majority of seats is simply an improbable miracle. I am ready to stake my reputation in affirming that no such miracle took place.

It is hard to escape the conclusion that the results of the elections which we have just had, had not been carefully programmed in advance. In any case, what we can note here again is that it is not at all easy to transform a dictatorship into a democracy using peaceful democratic methods. If we really want to, we must not despair, should not give up and should continue trying in all peaceful ways possible until we succeed because what is at stake is our collective survival and well-being. From the point of view of rationality, these elections ought to be cancelled and redone more carefully, fairly and transparently. We should even be ready to suppress our national pride and invite foreigners to help us organise them. What can be said with confidence is that our situation and lot is not likely to improve until genuine democracy which respects the will of the majority comes in one way or another. Meanwhile, we can only hope and pray that we do not get catapulted into the way of Rwanda, Burundi or former Zaire. But fear of civil war should not make us to accept the unacceptable. We should never again accept fraud and blatant injustice as we did in the past. In spite of the fraud *before* and *during* the elections, the advance propaganda of the CRTV clearly shows that there are plans not to announce the true results obtained at the polls and that we are about to start reliving 1992. This should not be allowed to happen.

Written 19/05/1997, published Monday, May 26, 1997.

31

Waiting for Kabila

Y ou may think I am referring to Mobutu. His Excellency Marshall Sese Seko Desire Mobutu, the erstwhile richest and most powerful dictator in all of central Africa, waited for two good days on board a ship in the Atlantic for his namesake, Desire Laurent Kabila, but the latter gave a flimsy excuse and did not show up. Mobutu waited in vain for Godot, drank his pride and returned without accomplishing his mission. It was already clear that power had deserted him and changed hands and that Kabila was now the one calling the shots, dictating the tune and setting both the pace and tempo of events. Every dictator, no matter how formidable, must kiss the dust, sooner or later. Where is Ahidjo today whom, less than two decades ago, Cameroonians worshipped as God? Where is Idi Amin of Uganda today, who once told the Queen of England "In England, you are the top man and, in Uganda, I am the top man"? One day, the village school teacher, Mwalimu Julius Nyerere, got fed up with Field Marshall Idi Amin's dictatorial antics and sent a handful of boys across the border to chase the monster out of Uganda. Where is Emperor Bedel Bokassa, of the former Central African Empire today? Where is the "'President for Life" of Malawi, Kamuzu Banda, today? They all kissed the dust. Of course, every human being must, sooner or later, "embrace the red earth." But then, not every human being pretends to be God. This inevitable fact is only pathetically pitiable in the case of those who have spent their lives trying to play God, trying, in vain, to be God.

People do not learn from history. Even new dictator hopes to be the one who, by being more clever, would reign *per omnia secula seculorum*. They fail to see how happy and preeminent, how highly respected everywhere, is someone like Julius Nyerere, for having wielded power gently and humbly and, most importantly, for giving up power voluntarily when he had all the means at his disposal to continue clinging on to it. One other such eminent personality on the African continent is Olusegun Obasanjo who is now languishing in Sani Abacha's jail. Obasanjo is respected and revered everywhere because, as a military strong man, he actually did hand over power to a civilian administration democratically elected, even though the idea and programme of handing over were not his but that of his assassinated charismatic predecessor Murtala Muhammad.

There is a Kabila for every Mobutu and a day of reckoning for every dictator. The day will come like a joke or a thief at night when least expected. On that day, the dictator will abandon his marble palaces in the country he considered his personal property, pack his personal effects and immediate family in his personal jets and head for his marble palaces in foreign lands. Associate dictators, surrogates and collaborators would suddenly find the ground under their feet, which they thought so solid and firm, giving way with dramatic immediacy. It would be time to board a boat across the river to an uncertain future in a neighbouring country. At such a time, how envious they would be of the common man on the street, the real proprietor of legitimate power, who has nowhere else to go and doesn't have to go anywhere!

It is very instructive to learn that the Swiss have decided to freeze all of Mobutu's coded accounts in Swiss banks, estimated at billions of US dollars! This is stolen money they received for safe keeping, knowing fully well that it was stolen money. Why did they have to wait until the fellow was overthrown before confiscating the stolen wealth? Will they return it to the rightful owners? Your guess is as good as mine. But, this very first step of seizing the stolen wealth should be a signal to the other Mobutus, as they dread the coming of Kabila, the inevitable eschatological day of reckoning. Kabila could, of course, turn out to be a false messiah. I have already offered my own personal advice as to how he can be a genuine one. But whether false or genuine, Kabila will come.

Our own Kabila may not yet have been born but that is not to say that he has not yet been conceived. In any case, we are at the end of all moral and rational procedural options and have no other choice than waiting for Kabila. We have to accept the fact that we have remained under the sway of the CNU/CPDM one party system, in spite of rhetoric to the contrary. The combination of democratic rhetoric and play-acting with dictatorial practice is Cameroon's peculiar and very dangerous contribution to political theory and practice in our epoch. It is really bizzare to hear HE Paul Biya, in his capacity as out-going Chairman of the OAU, hypocritically but qualmlessly calling for democratisation in Africa! Given the linkage between provincial Governors, *Préfets, Sous-Préfets,* the armed forces, and the sundry evil geniuses benefitting from the situation and their collective fanatical determination to maintain the *status quo,* there does not appear to be any formula by which our monolithic dictatorship can ever be changed into a genuine democracy using peaceful democratic methods. And so we have no option but to wait for Kabila. We are far from salvation and waiting for the messiah. Let us wait in humility and prayerful hope. Amen!

Written 25/05/97, published Monday, June 2, 1997.

32

Kleptocracy and Mendacity as Identification Marks

The unmistakable identification marks of the political regime which is co-extensive with the Ahidjo dictatorship without being identical with it are *kleptocracy* and *mendacity* or in plainer English, stealing and lying. I hope that asserting a difference or distinction within what is co-extensive is in no way problematic, for a continuous entity may, nevertheless, have significant qualitative differences in its spatial or temporal extensions or parts. I have before characterised the Ahidjo end of the single continuous entity under review as pre-eminently dictatorial, but that is no longer our problem except in the sense that what is now our problem is its direct legacy which can be viewed as Ahidjo's curse on Cameroonians. Does all that sound like the preamble to an inaugural lecture? This is no inaugural lecture but something quite banal and mundane that I am saying.

Until I read Boh Herbert's piece entitled *"A l'ecran cette semaine: le retour de Zero mort"* in *L' EXPRESSION* N0, 125 of Monday 26 May 1997, I had forgotten the complete catalogue of incredible lies *officially* told to Cameroonians and the world at large through the mouth-piece of the New Deal regime. Whatever regime will succeed in succeeding the New Deal will have an uphill task restoring the confidence of Cameroonians in democratic processes and in the statements, pronouncements and declarations of the government. This is, by far, the greatest damage that has been done to our body politic. Government is indispensable in all human societies. And to have a human society whose members justifiably have no confidence in its rulers is a very serious matter indeed, a consequence of prolonged systematic mendacity and thievery.

Regarding the first term of our title, there is a remarkable story that I have never yet told but which still makes me to chuckle sadly every time I recall it. It happened in 1993 or thereabouts and, if you doubt its authenticity, you can confirm its veracity from *Taadom*

Saultan who used to write a column under that same rubric in *Cameroon Post* in its heyday. Taadom Saultan was a participant ear and eye witness to the remarkable story you are about to read.

One day, Taadom Saultan gave me a lift in his car from Bamenda to Yaounde. The other people in the car were his wife and two little kids and a young nephew of his, about 5 years old, with the unusual name of Aquinas. Throughout the journey, I was very "pissed off" with Aquinas because I was very anxious to get to Yaounde as quickly as possible whereas, every few kilometres, the little "yamhead" said that he wanted to shit. I didn't ask him if he knew the *past tense of shit* because we were not communicating in English but rather in local Russian. However, the point is that whenever Taadom stopped for Aquinas to shit, he would come out of the car but then refuse to shit. But, no sooner the journey resumed, than he would start pleading again in his little pathetic voice that he wanted to shit. By the time Taadom had stopped for the third time for Aquinas to shit, and he came out and refused to shit, I was really in a rage and could have caned him had a cane been handy.

Then we crossed the Sanaga and started overtaking the sand-carrying lorries in hussed concentration. Taadom, at a point, remarked that when you are driving from Yaounde to Bamenda, you usually find yourself at the Sanaga in no time but that, when coming from Bamenda to Yaounde, after crossing the Sanaga, you would always seem to be chasing Yaounde indefinitely while it seems ever to be receding.

At long last, *Unity Palace* appeared on the horizon and we heaved a sigh of relief. Taadom addressed Aquinas:

> "Aquinas, look at that big house on top of the hill there. Do you know who Paul Biya is?"
> "Yes," answered Aquinas confidently. "Who is he?" pursued Taadom, expecting the answer "the President of Cameroon" so that he could then teach him that, that is where he lives and that it is called "The Presidency of the Republic or Unity Palace."

But Aquinas cleared his little throat and, in his slightly pathetic but clear voice, answered:

"He is a thief!"
"What?" Taadom and I shouted in unison, "You say Paul Biya is who?"
"A thief" he repeated clearly and confidently.

We all had what might be described as an attack of laughter during which the car nearly skidded off the road. When the first phase of laughter subsided, I wanted to recheck the veracity of my senses, so I turned to Aquinas on the back seat:

"Aquinas, *dji a suiy dji Paul Biya dze laa?*"
(You say Paul Biya is who?)
"*Dze shong*" (A thief), he reconfirmed, unhesitatingly and confidently.

We laughed from Etoudi right to Mendong and, when we arrived, people thought we were bringing news of death from home because of the copious tears flowing from all our eyes. I had to forgive Aquinas for all his earlier shitty stuff.

I have never been able to find out how a young child came by such a devastating opinion. Maybe you have an idea. But in the domain of election victories alone, it is not at all an implausible opinion. Or what do you think?

This is the 32nd edition of *IN THE SPIRIT*. The 33rd edition will hum a provisional *non-dimitis*.

Written 03/06/1997, published Monday, June 16, 1997.

33

Non Dimittis, Domine

M an plans and God unplans. I had planned to sing my *nunc dimittis* about now. You remember Simeon, don't you? Yes, the Simeon of the New Testament, "the upright and devout man" of Jerusalem who witnessed Jesus' "presentation in the temple." You can read that remarkable story in Luke Chapter Two, or don't you have a bible? God had promised Pa Simeon that he would not die until he had seen the Messiah. So, when Pa took the Saviour in his arms, he was overwhelmed with joy and praised and thanked God saying:

> Now, Lord, you may discharge and dismiss your servant, for I don't mind dying, now that my own eyes have seen the salvation which you promised to your long suffering people.

I had begged God not to let me relax my commitment, not to discharge and release me from my self-imposed duty and not to let me die until I had seen democracy, meritocracy, fair play and justice in Cameroon. I had planned to chant my *nunc dimittis* about now when we all expected a new and truly democratic parliament would be inaugurated, ending three decades of two successive dictatorships. But who would have imagined that the New Deal dictatorship of His Excellency Paul Beer, and its evil geniuses, surrogates and associates, would demonstrate such Machiavellian cleverness in subverting the democratic struggle and hanging on to power? So, instead of singing my *nunc dimittis*, I am now forced to sing: *NON DIMITTIS, DOMINO*. May the Lord not discharge me or allow me to die before the coming of Kabila, before the advent and victorious triumph of him who will deliver us from the strangulating grip of a band of hardened criminals who fear neither man nor God.

Had we had our democratic breakthrough and had I been able to chant my *nunc dimittis*, I would have dropped my pen for good and you would not ever read Gobata again on the pages of any newspaper, though you would surely read him between the covers of some books. This is the 33rd edition of *IN THE SPIRIT*, a sacred number we can respect with a pause. So this will be a pause and not a termination, a comma (,) and not a full stop (.). This column will resume in exactly the same format and under the same rubric in the very foreseeable future.

During the interim, if anyone starts telling you that Gobata has gone on exile, know that that is patently false, that your informant is a liar. Gobata is not the exile-going type. Why should I go on exile when those who ought to go on exile for having destroyed this beautiful country are gambolling around cockily with the air of private owners of this rough triangle? Those who were speculating during my last meditative retreat that I had gone on exile have not read Gobata or have read without understanding. During this pause, I will be available, if anyone wants to see me eye to eye. If you reach Djoungolo and ask anybody, even any small pickin, s/he will show you my favourite *Off-License* where I usually quench my thirst, or even bring you to my domicile. Whenever I will resume this column, even if it is through a different medium, know that I am the one and don't believe those who will be suggesting that someone else is trying to impersonate Gobata. Those who really know me cannot mistake anyone else for me anywhere or at any time. I have my equals and betters, but no one can successfully impersonate Gobata while I am still breathing, unless and until such a person has received and is thoroughly imbued and suffused with *the spirit of Gobata. A daughter of the son of Gobata* is in the process of being groomed, but it will take more than a decade before she starts her public ministry.

So I will surely be back, sooner than later, to continue crying out for democracy and meritocracy, for justice and fair play. I will be back to continue denouncing, without equivocation, without fear of favour, dictatorship and mediocrity, fraud and thievery, injustice and foul play. Until ... the advent of the Saviour, the coming of Kabila;... until we see salvation. In the interim, I will seize the opportunity to redress certain mundacities connected with this column. All my life, I have striven for a certain order and tidiness in all I do. I detest everything that is irremediably nebulous and/or foggy and/or unclear. I love operating from clear principles and rules of procedure. 1 believe in *trial -and-error-elimination* as the only way by which a fallible being, that I am, that we all are, can make any progress in the world, but I do not believe in *trial- and-error* as a method of work. These mundane, but, nevertheless, important issues would surely have been thrashed out by the time *IN THE SPIRIT* resumes.

But, should God unplan my plans, let me say here (in advance) what I usually say at the end of each and all of my personal love relationships: *IT WAS SO GOOD WHILE IT LASTED!*

Lastly, a word of advice to the genuine opposition parties, especially the SDF and UNDP. This is a very hard moment of decision. You have been flagrantly cheated and robbed of victory (again!) as in 1992. My well considered and honest advice in this situation is as follows:

> Do not boycott the parliament. Make it clear to everybody that you are *not_*going in there *because* you accept the fraudulent results of the elections, and then go in. The struggle should continue from within there and from without. We would like to believe that there are no non-patriots among your elected parliamentarians Outside the Assembly, we, ordinary Cameroonians, should engage in weekly demonstrations all over the national territory, for the creation of a credible *independent electoral commission.* The presidential elections are only a few months away. They will be crucial and decisive and they hold the last hope of bringing change to this God-forsaken country. The CPDM is condemned to field Beer. Should they decide to field someone else, that would be even worse for them, because that would surely split them right up the centre. I don't know of any other prospect for which ordinary Cameroonians would prefer death than the prospect of having Beer for seven more years. With a unique opposition

candidate, victory for the democratic forces, for the long-suffering masses, would be a certainly under all conceivable possible scenarios. Please, don't treat this proposal with levity. God be with us! Amen and Goodbye.

Written 10/06/1997, published Friday, June 20, 1997.

Titles by *Langaa* RPCIG

Francis B. Nyamnjoh
Stories from Abakwa
Mind Searching
The Disillusioned African
The Convert
Souls Forgotten
Married But Available
Intimate Strangers

Dibussi Tande
No Turning Back. Poems of Freedom 1990-1993
Scribbles from the Den: Essays on Politics and Collective
Memory in Cameroon

Kangsen Feka Wakai
Fragmented Melodies

Ntemfac Ofege
Namondo. Child of the Water Spirits
Hot Water for the Famous Seven

Emmanuel Fru Doh
Not Yet Damascus
The Fire Within
Africa's Political Wastelands: The Bastardization of Cameroon
Oriki'badan
Wading the Tide
Stereotyping Africa: Surprising Answers to Surprising Questions

Thomas Jing
Tale of an African Woman

Peter Wuteh Vakunta
Grassfields Stories from Cameroon
Green Rape: Poetry for the Environment
Majunga Tok: Poems in Pidgin English
Cry, My Beloved Africa
No Love Lost
Straddling The Mungo: A Book of Poems in English
& French

Ba'bila Mutia
Coils of Mortal Flesh

Kehbuma Langmia
Titabet and the Takumbeng
An Evil Meal of Evil
The Earth Mother

Victor Elame Musinga
The Bam
The Tragedy of Mr. No Balance

Ngessimo Mathe Mutaka
Building Capacity: Using TEFL and African Languages as
Development-oriented Literacy Tools

Milton Krieger
Cameroon's Social Democratic Front: Its History and Prospects as
an Opposition Political Party, 1990-2011

Sammy Oke Akombi
The Raped Amulet
The Woman Who Ate Python
Beware the Drives: Book of Verse
The Wages of Corruption

Susan Nkwentie Nde
Precipice
Second Engagement

Francis B. Nyamnjoh & Richard Fonteh Akum
The Cameroon GCE Crisis: A Test of Anglophone Solidarity

Joyce Ashuntantang & Dibussi Tande
Their Champagne Party Will End! Poems in Honor of Bate
Besong

Emmanuel Achu
Disturbing the Peace

Rosemary Ekosso
The House of Falling Women

Peterkins Manyong
God the Politician

George Ngwane
The Power in the Writer: Collected Essays on Culture, Democracy
& Development in Africa

John Percival
The 1961 Cameroon Plebiscite: Choice or Betrayal

Albert Azeyeh
Réussite scolaire, faillite sociale : généalogie mentale de la crise
de l'Afrique noire francophone

Aloysius Ajab Amin & Jean-Luc Dubois
Croissance et développement au Cameroun :
d'une croissance équilibrée à un développement équitable

Carlson Anyangwe
Imperialistic Politics in Cameroun:
Resistance & the Inception of the Restoration of the Statehood
of Southern Cameroons
Betrayal of Too Trusting a People: The UN, the UK and the Trust
Territory of the Southen Cameroons

Bill F. Ndi
K'Cracy, Trees in the Storm and Other Poems
Map: Musings On Ars Poetica
Thomas Lurting: The Fighting Sailor Turn'd Peaceable /Le marin
combattant devenu paisible
Soleil et ombre

**Kathryn Toure, Therese Mungah
Shalo Tchombe & Thierry Karsenti**
ICT and Changing Mindsets in Education

Charles Alobwed'Epie
The Day God Blinked
The Bad Samaritan
The Lady with the Sting
What a Next of Kin!

G. D. Nyamndi
Babi Yar Symphony
Whether losing, Whether winning
Tussles: Collected Plays
Dogs in the Sun

Samuel Ebelle Kingue
Si Dieu était tout un chacun de nous ?

Ignasio Malizani Jimu
Urban Appropriation and Transformation: bicycle, taxi and
handcart operators in Mzuzu, Malawi

Justice Nyo' Wakai
Under the Broken Scale of Justice: The Law and My Times

John Eyong Mengot
A Pact of Ages

Ignasio Malizani Jimu
Urban Appropriation and Transformation: Bicycle Taxi and
Handcart Operators

Joyce B. Ashuntantang
Landscaping and Coloniality: The Dissemination of Cameroon
Anglophone Literature
A Basket of Flaming Ashes

Jude Fokwang
Mediating Legitimacy: Chieftaincy and Democratisation in Two
African Chiefdoms

Michael A. Yanou
Dispossession and Access to Land in South Africa:
an African Perspevctive

Tikum Mbah Azonga
Cup Man and Other Stories
The Wooden Bicycle and Other Stories

John Nkemngong Nkengasong
Letters to Marions (And the Coming Generations)
The Call of Blood

Amady Aly Dieng
Les étudiants africains et la littérature négro-africaine d'expression
française

Tah Asongwed
Born to Rule: Autobiography of a life President
Child of Earth

Frida Menkan Mbunda
Shadows From The Abyss

Bongasu Tanla Kishani
A Basket of Kola Nuts
Konglanjo (Spears of Love without Ill-fortune) and Letters to
Ethiopia with some Random Poems

Fo Angwafo III S.A.N of Mankon
Royalty and Politics: The Story of My Life

Basil Diki
The Lord of Anomy
Shrouded Blessings

Churchill Ewumbue-Monono
Youth and Nation-Building in Cameroon: A Study of National
Youth Day Messages and Leadership Discourse (1949-2009)

Emmanuel N. Chia, Joseph C. Suh & Alexandre Ndeffo Tene
Perspectives on Translation and Interpretation in Cameroon

Linus T. Asong
The Crown of Thorns
No Way to Die
A Legend of the Dead: Sequel of *The Crown of Thorns*
The Akroma File
Salvation Colony: Sequel to *No Way to Die*
Chopchair
Doctor Frederick Ngenito
The Crabs of Bangui

Vivian Sihshu Yenika
Imitation Whiteman
Press Lake Varsity Girls: The Freshman Year

Beatrice Fri Bime
Someplace, Somewhere
Mystique: A Collection of Lake Myths

Shadrach A. Ambanasom
Son of the Native Soil
The Cameroonian Novel of English Expression:
An Introduction
Education of the Deprived: Anglophone Cameroon Literary
Drama
Homage and Courtship *(Romantic Stirrings of a Young Man)*

Tangie Nsoh Fonchingong and Gemandze John Bobuin
Cameroon: The Stakes and Challenges of Governance and
Development

Tatah Mentan
Democratizing or Reconfiguring Predatory Autocracy? Myths and
Realities in Africa Today

Roselyne M. Jua & Bate Besong
To the Budding Creative Writer: A Handbook

Albert Mukong
Prisonner without a Crime: Disciplining Dissent in Ahidjo's
Cameroon

Mbuh Tennu Mbuh
In the Shadow of my Country

Bernard Nsokika Fonlon
Genuine Intellectuals: Academic and Social Responsibilities of
Universities in Africa

Lilian Lem Atanga
Gender, Discourse and Power in the Cameroonian Parliament

Cornelius Mbifung Lambi & Emmanuel Neba Ndenecho
Ecology and Natural Resource Development
in the Western Highlands of Cameroon: Issues in Natural Resource
Managment

Gideon F. For-mukwai
Facing Adversity with Audacity

Peter W. Vakunta & Bill F. Ndi
Nul n'a le monopole du français : deux poètes du Cameroon
anglophone

Emmanuel Matateyou
Les murmures de l'harmattan

Ekpe Inyang
The Hill Barbers

JK Bannavti
Rock of God *(Kilán ke Nyùy)*

Godfrey B. Tangwa (Rotcod Gobata)
I Spit on their Graves: Testimony Relevant to the Democratization
Struggle in Cameroon
Road Companion to Democracy and Meritocracy *(Further Essays
from an African Perspective)*

Henrietta Mambo Nyamnjoh
"We Get Nothing from Fishishing", Fishing for Boat Opportunies
amongst Senegalese Fisher Migrants

Bill F. Ndi, Dieurat Clervoyant & Peter W. Vakunta
Les douleurs de la plume noire : du Cameroun anglophone à Haïti

Laurence Juma
Kileleshwa: A Tale of Love, Betrayal and Corruption in Kenya

Nol Alembong
Forest Echoes (Poems)

Marie-Hélène Mottin-Sylla & Joëlle Palmieri
Excision : les jeunes changent l'Afrique par les TIC

Walter Gam Nkwi
Voicing the Voiceless: Contributions to Closing Gaps in
Cameroon History, 1958-2009

John Koyela Fokwang
A Dictionary of Popular Bali Names

Alain-Joseph Sissao
(Translated from the French by Nina Tanti)
Folktales from the Moose of Burkina Faso

Colin Ayeab Diyen
The Earth in Peril